How to Sell
and Manage in
Tough Times and
Tough Markets

Tom Reilly

How to Sell and Manage in Tough Times and Tough Markets

Relief for salespeople and managers

Tom Reilly

Published by
Motivation Press
St. Louis

Library of Congress Cataloging in Publication Data

Reilly, Thomas P.
  How to Sell and Manage in Tough Times and Tough Markets
  Tom Reilly
  ISBN: 0-944448-22-4

Other Books by Tom Reilly:
  Value Added Selling
  Value Added Sales Management
  Value Added Customer Service
  Simple Psychology
  Selling Smart
  Crush Price Objections
  The Value Added Organization

Copyright © 2001 by Tom Reilly
Library of Congress Catalog Card Number: 2001093028
International Standard Book Number: 0-944448-22-4

Printed in the United States of America by Motivation Press.

Dedication

To Andrew, my son,
who has faced more tough times
than most people I know.
I am proud to have him call me Dad.

Acknowledgements

I wish to thank my staff—Joann, Linda, and Charlotte—for their help in producing this book on an incredible publishing deadline. I especially wish to thank Joann Hamilton for her Herculean efforts in producing this book.

Table of Contents

The Young Eagle
By Tom Reilly

The nest of young eagles hung on every word as the Master Eagle described his exploits. This was an important day for the eaglets. They were preparing for their first solo flight from the nest. It was the confidence builder many of them needed to fulfill their destiny.

"How *far* can I travel?" asked one of the eaglets.

"How far can you *see*?" responded the Master Eagle.

"How *high* can I fly?" quizzed the young eagle.

"How far can you *stretch your wings*?" asked the old eagle.

"How *long* can I fly?" the eaglet persisted.

"How far is the *horizon*?" the mentor rebounded.

"How much *should* I dream?" asked the eaglet.

"How much *can* you dream?" smiled the older, wiser eagle.

"How much can I *achieve*?" the young one continued.

"How much can you *believe*?" the old eagle challenged.

Frustrated by the banter, the young eagle demanded, "Why don't you answer my questions?"

"I did."

"Yes. But you answered them with questions."

"I answered them the best I could."

"But you're the Master Eagle. You're supposed to know everything. If you can't answer these questions, who can?"

"You." the old, wise eagle reassured.

"Me? How?" the young eagle was confused.

"No one can tell you how high to fly or how much to dream. It's different for each eagle. Only you and God know how far you'll go. No one on this earth knows your potential or what's in your heart. You alone will answer that. The only thing that limits you is the edge of your imagination."

The young eagle, puzzled by this, asked, "What should I do?"

"Look to the horizon, spread your wings, and fly."

Introduction

It was the best of times, it was the worst of times,
it was the age of wisdom, it was the age of foolishness,
it was the epoch of belief, it was the epoch of incredulity,
it was the season of Light, it was the season of Darkness,
it was the spring of hope, it was the winter of despair . . .
Charles Dickens, A Tale of Two Cities

Even though Charles Dickens wrote this in the mid-nineteenth century about a different time and a distant place, the French Revolution, he could have been writing about the dramatic shift in the U.S. economy at the dawn of the new millennium. For some, this economy is "the best of times"; for others, it is "the worst of times." Wall Street went from the "season of Light" to the "season of Darkness." In the midst of the current economic uncertainty, there are those who look to the future with great trepidation; for them, it is the "winter of despair." Others look to the future through the eyes of an optimist; for them, it is the "spring of hope."

That some people are able to maintain a positive focus and perform admirably and successfully, regardless of the conditions that surround their efforts, has always fascinated me. Faced with identical circumstances, some people rise to the challenge, tapping into the "best" in themselves, and achieve what others cannot even imagine. Consider this: In tough times, 25% of businesses fail, 70% survive, and 5% thrive.

On a broader scale, some people play the cards they are dealt while other people fold 'em and go home. Some people thrive on the challenge; others wilt in the heat of battle. The resilience of the human spirit is nature's way of equipping us with the fuel we need to soar above whatever obstacles we encounter.

Even though I began this project to help salespeople and their managers successfully navigate turbulent waters, I serendipitously discovered that those things which help salespeople and managers thrive in tough times can help anyone from any walk of life confront their adversities with courage and direction.

Whether they rebounded from a business failure, survived a POW camp, or recovered from a life-threatening illness, every successful person I know has fought a major battle and won. They emerged victorious from strife, a graduate from the University of Adversity. When people discover the hidden strength within them to rise above adversity, they are forever changed by the experience. The strength they used to face adversity, they now summon for use in good times. This book is about the attitudes and strategies salespeople and managers can use to emerge victorious from tough times and tough markets. Although you may apply these ideas to other areas in your life, *How to Sell and Manage in Tough Times and Tough Markets* is a business book.

I began this research in 1990. We were on the verge of another economic downturn. The U.S. had just rebounded from a deep recession in the early eighties, and the pundits were beginning to see signs of economic turmoil on the horizon. I scoured through mountains of trade journal articles, newspaper stories, and business publications to find any information I could pass along to my clients in seminars to give them hope for tough times. I interviewed successful business owners who seemed to shrug off tough times as an amusing anecdote about their markets that did not apply to them. I surveyed salespeople and their buyers to discover what was on their minds. I even relied on my background in psychology to help me formulate a model to help my customers through tough times.

I tested these ideas with clients and they worked. People liked what they heard. I continued to amass information over the years, and the result of those efforts is the book you are reading. These practical ideas, laced with personal experiences of tough times, offer a multifaceted perspective on how to thrive in tough times.

Consider this . . .

* Troubled adolescence,
* Fought in war at age nineteen,
* Lost parents way too early in life,
* Began sales career in a commodity industry,
* Worked full time and attended college full time to graduate in 3½ years,
* Started new business while attending graduate school to earn a Master's Degree,
* Started and ran two successful businesses during recessions,
* Lost voice to cancer at age thirty,
* Business was devastated in the Great Flood of 1993.

These are a few of the challenges I have confronted through the years. What's the point? I share these with you, not in a self-aggrandizing manner, but to establish some personal credibility for this topic. I am not comfortable sharing these events with other people; I don't like picking my scabs in public. If these sound self-inflating, I apologize. I simply wish to illustrate a point. *Everyone* deals with adversity. There is no escape from it. How you choose to deal with your adversities determines whether you emerge as victor or victim. And there isn't much future in being a victim.

Many of you reading this book have dealt with adversities far greater than anything I've experienced in my lifetime. Some have emerged from these experiences battle-scarred and victorious; others have submitted to fortune's will. As a friend of mine is fond of saying, "The hardest steel comes from the hottest fire." One of life's stark realities is that all people confront adversity; one of life's richest blessings is that each of us has within us the power to confront adversity with courage and determination. We do have a choice in how we fight this battle. No one makes us a victim without our permission.

Since 1981, I've had the privilege of working with some of the best organizations in the world. Many are world-class leaders in their industries. These companies range from Fortune-500 manufacturers to small distributors and service providers in a variety of industries: construction, industrial goods, financial institutions, heavy-duty trucking, automotive, healthcare, textiles, consulting services, food service, and petroleum, to name a few. I've learned as much from them as I've taught them. I was their student as well as their teacher, and I took a lot of notes along the way.

As one company struggles to keeps its doors open during tough times, another company faced with equally challenging circumstances hires more people, invests in new technology, and surrounds customers with the message that they will ride out the storm together and things will get better. One emerges from adversity ready for growth; the other limps out of adversity, losing ground. Those companies focused on survival contract as the economy contracts; they cut and slash and hunker down to weather the storm. Those companies intent on thriving in tough times follow a contrarian philosophy of expansion during economic contraction; they invest and expand and surge forward, as if they had a mandate to grow—they refuse to participate in the recession.

I look at these two companies and see fundamental differences in management style and company philosophy. The victorious company is led by a strong management team that has weathered many storms. These battle-hardened veterans learned valuable lessons and prepared for tough times. The struggling company is led by a weak management team that learned nothing from previous challenges and failed to prepare for tough times.

How to Sell and Manage in Tough Times and Tough Markets is a book for salespeople and their managers. By reading this book and applying these ideas, you will learn how to thrive—not just survive—in tough times. Tough times brings out more of who you are. If you are a strong person, you will witness great strength in tough times. If you are weak, your weakness will be your greatest adversary in tough times. A persistent and intentionally redundant theme throughout this book is that you have a choice for how you want to behave in tough times: *You may not be able to control the outcome of your circumstances, but you can control your input.*

This book is filled with dozens of practical, how-to tips and motivational thoughts. My mission is to inform and to inspire. Even though the focus is business, you will discover that many of these ideas have broad application for other areas in life where you face tough challenges. Learning how to effectively deal with tough times raises your confidence level and your competence level. The downside of failing to learn these lessons is that you allow yourself to wallow in misery that serves no purpose other than to keep you miserable. If this book helps you to stop and think before cutting prices, builds your confidence for confronting tough times, or inspires you to move forward, I've accomplished my goal.

I've organized this book into five chapters. Chapter 1 provides you with background information on tough times and some historical perspective. I define terms, discuss the biggest mistakes salespeople make in tough times, what buyers really want from sellers, what buyers worry about in tough times, and the competitive realities of selling in tough times.

Chapter 2 deals with the mental side of tough times. Half the battle is in your head, and the other half is on the streets. I discuss positive and negative attitudes, the characteristics of people who do well in tough times, and positive mental programming tips.

Chapter 3 is for salespeople. I discuss behind-the-scenes and face-to-face selling tips for tough times. These field-tested and street-smart ideas give you the hope and help you need to persist when the economy is soft.

Chapter 4 is for managers. This includes the four biggest mistakes that managers make in tough times and seventeen things managers must do to effectively lead their organizations in and out of tough times. Employees and customers look to managers for leadership in tough times. This chapter prepares you for the leadership challenge.

Chapter 5 is closing thoughts. In this, I recap the dominant themes of this book and offer thoughts for the future.

When I think about tough times and what it takes to rebound—to get up each morning, lick your wounds, and go out into the world for another go at it—I like to reflect on Abraham Lincoln and his challenges in life:

1831 - failed in business

1832 - defeated for legislature

1833 - failed a second time in business

1836 - suffered a nervous breakdown

1838 - defeated for speaker

1840 - defeated for elector

1843 - defeated for Congress

1848 - defeated for Congress again

1855 - defeated for Senate

1856 - defeated for Vice President

1858 - defeated for Senate again

1860 - elected President of the United States

Lincoln took the helm of a country that was on a collision course of civil war. His greatest challenge was to preserve the Union, at any cost. When you consider the incredible challenges he faced throughout his life, you can see that all of these disappointments conditioned him for the toughest job any President of the United States would ever face.

What makes his story more compelling is that during his presidency, he faced great adversity in his personal and professional life. From impotent generals to personal tragedy to disloyal aides, Lincoln rose above it all, preserved the integrity of the Union, and steered the country back on course to becoming the greatest nation in the history of the world.

Had he quit, one could only speculate the destiny of the United States and the rest of the world today. His example serves as a beacon for what the human spirit can endure in life's darkest moments. For his efforts, our nation owes him a debt of gratitude. As humans, we can draw strength from his example. As business people, we can learn from his persuasiveness, patience, and leadership.

1
Introduction to Tough Times

Nothing succeeds like success.
Alexander Dumas
Nothing succeeds like excess.
Oscar Wilde
Nothing recedes like success.
Walter Winchell

Since 1854, we have experienced thirty-two economic downturns in the United States, each lasting about 1½ years, followed by an expansion of about three years. It seems we've discovered a way to handle these downturns more effectively, because over the past forty years, the average contraction is less than one year and the average expansion is almost four years. If you work in sales and management long enough, you will experience a downturn.

What are tough times?

Tough times happen when you have an extended period of declining economic activity. The dictionary defines a recession as, "a temporary falling off of business activity during a period when such activity has been generally increasing."

The United States government defines a recession as two consecutive quarters of negative economic growth.

Economists call it tough times when key economic indicators are down: housing starts, employment statistics, Gross Domestic Product, and wages stagnate; other indicators are up: inflation, interest rates, layoffs, fuel and energy prices, trade deficits, and the consumer price index.

In business terms, tough times exist when supply is greater than demand, creating the proverbial buyer's market. The economy may be steaming along at a great pace, but if it's a buyer's market, you're experiencing tough times. It's a different kind of tough times when demand is greater than supply. It's a seller's market. Even though it sounds great, it brings another set of problems for salespeople: backorders, product allocation, irate customers, stressed and overworked staff, and restricted growth.

All downturns share some common denominators. Companies reduce their inventory levels, cut production, and implement cost containment programs. Unemployment increases and consumers reduce spending.

> ➤ If your neighbor is out of work, it's a recession; if you're out of work, it's a depression.

It's tough times when you must work harder to tread water—you find it difficult to get ahead. It doesn't have to be a full-blown recession to be tough times. If your company can't ship products for whatever reason, it's tough times.

Anyone who has ever been through the start-up of a new facility can relate to tough times. Any new venture contains its own wrinkles, which makes life tougher for salespeople. Starting a new business with limited funds is tough times; you're attempting to accomplish a lot with a little. Dealing with the residue of natural disasters presents a unique blend of tough times issues. Construction of a new facility may wreak havoc on a business if it pushes deadlines and budgets. Times are tough when businesses cannot hire enough qualified workers to get the job done.

Tough times are not limited to recessions or broad-based economic slowdowns. They occur in as many ways as people feel stress and pressure. Talk to any parent who has several children in college at the same time; they understand tough times. Change, by its nature, presents tough times for some people.

When I was in school, a friend of mine broke both of his arms and couldn't drive, carry his books, or attend to some of nature's most fundamental necessities. The economy was fine, but his world was turned upside-down for a while. He accepted the reality of his situation and adapted to it. He made it through his tough times and did just fine. In the process, he learned something about the tough times attitude that has served him well later in life. He has owned a business for years and weathered many storms in a volatile industry. I believe he learned something different from each storm that prepared him for the next one.

On a recent trip to California, the hotel I stayed in had a note card on the dresser in my room asking guests to be "energy conscious." They explained the necessity of the energy surcharge on the hotel bill. This state is experiencing an energy crisis, their energy costs have doubled. If you're a small company that depends heavily on energy for your livelihood and you live in California, you're experiencing tough times, regardless of the rest of the economy.

Tough times appear in as many ways as there are people and events. It's wasted energy to compare the magnitude of your tough times with someone else's. The only emotions that result from comparing yourself to other people is that you become smug or frustrated—neither of which helps you deal effectively with tough times.

Tough markets

In Greek mythology, Sisyphus was condemned to push a boulder up a hill in Hades for eternity. Just as he would get close to the top of the hill, the boulder would roll down the hill and he would have to start over. Most salespeople

I've met say they feel as if they were Sisyphus and their sales quotas are their boulders. It's a never-ending struggle to reach an ever-increasing sales quota.

If you have strong competitors who sell quality products, at competitive prices, with good service, you're in a tough market. Most companies I work with grossly underestimate the strength of their competitors. All markets are tough. No one has a lock on tough industries. Many people believe their markets are unique and the toughest of any industry. Even salespeople in the same company compare their territories with their peers and brag about who has the toughest territory.

There are rolling recessions—tough times that roll from one industry to another or one geographic area to another. It may be the heavy-duty truck industry today, the chemical industry tomorrow, and the construction industry a year from now. When Boeing moves its headquarters from Seattle to Chicago, it's tough times for Seattle and great times for Chicago. One man's pain is another man's pleasure. But in Seattle, there is a rollover effect to other industries that depend heavily on a company for their business. As they suffer, their siblings in Chicago prosper.

The domino effect of one company sneezing and the rest of the market catching a cold is recognized widely in business. The economy tightens and companies trim expenses. Travel is down. The airlines are affected and run special offers. Hotel occupancy rates are down a few points, and they decide to offer some special deals. Convention attendance is down, and the cab drivers and restaurants notice.

Companies further tighten their belts and cut back on printing, which means the paper and ink salespeople sell fewer products. And if the printers sit idle because of lower demand, they have no reason to buy new presses. The equipment salespeople suffer. In the midst and mire of all of this misery, one company sees discount airfares, cheap hotel rates, low printing costs, and perceives this as an opportunity to blitzkrieg their market with sales calls and new brochures.

> ➢ Some companies perceive opportunities where others see obstacles.

There are tough markets in every industry. The beer industry may have explosive growth in the west and southwest and flat sales in the north. I work with a company that has thirty branches. As of the writing of this book, twenty-five branches are enjoying good times and thriving. Five branches are struggling. When this book hits the market, those five branches will have rebounded only to have five other branches experience a downturn. This is the reality of the business world—it's not cynical, it's how things work.

The reality of business is that things ebb and flow, oftentimes as the result of events beyond the control of most businesses. The most you can hope to accomplish is to adapt to changing market conditions and move on. Some territories are tougher than others. Some regions of the country tend to be more price sensitive than others. Some product lines compete in markets and at price points that are more cutthroat than others.

I have witnessed great companies—known for their incredible service, quality, and value—with branch operations that are terrible compared to the other locations. It may be the management, their sales force, or market conditions out of their span of control. What's the point?

> ➢ Tough times and tough markets exist, and it's never fair. Accept it. Get used to it. Move on.

Hand wringing is grossly overrated. No one promised any of us that it would be easy to succeed in business. As Robert E. Lee advised his son, "Live in the world you inhabit. Look upon things as they are. Take them as you find them. Make the best of them. Turn them to your advantage." Use this pragmatic optimism as your gyroscope in choppy waters.

Tough times signals

During the Great Flood of '93, many people in our community courted disaster because of their denial of the possibility of a flood. My training center is located in the lowest spot of Chesterfield Valley—the center of the saucer.

When the levy broke, we eventually drew eleven feet of water. For a month prior to the flood, the levy suffered unprecedented boiling; water seeped under the levy and bubbled up on the other side. This was a sure-fire harbinger that the levy was weak in this spot. I can remember watching the bubbling get worse for a month, as others ignored the warning signs. Fortunately for me, I took some precautionary actions that helped me thrive when times got tough. Others who ignored the signals suffered much greater losses than I. We grew at an unprecedented rate of 35% that year, and we were out of our offices for four months!

> ➢ Being proactive means never having to say, "Gee, I wish I had done something about this before now."

There are a number of things that signal tough times on the horizon. Being aware of these and remaining vigilant will help you engage tough times successfully. Some of these are internal signals while others are external signals.

1. Internal signals

Your company has installed a hiring moratorium, they have frozen wages, and they are encouraging employees to take early retirements. Your company has slashed advertising dollars, travel expenses, and trade show budgets. You see a consolidation of departments. Your suppliers and potential suppliers call on your company more frequently. In my company, we knew things were beginning to contract as more printers, most of whom we didn't know, started calling on us in person and on the phone.

2. *External signals*

If you encounter more price resistance than you normally experience, it's a signal that things are tightening in your market. Buyers try to negotiate lower prices. That's a given in negotiating. What I'm referring to is price sensitivity born out of necessity for survival. Customers who tell you they have a mandate from management to curtail all expenses are sending you a strong signal of things to come. When Chrysler demands a 5% across-the-board price reduction from their suppliers, brace yourself; tough times are on the horizon. Price objections from satisfied customers are especially troublesome and ominous. Why would a completely satisfied customer, who recognizes your value, complain about price?

> ➢ Across industries, one out of six shoppers
> is a price shopper.

If you are not losing one out of six deals to price, you're probably too cheap to begin with. If you're losing more than one out of six, you may need to bone up on your selling skills, or things could be tightening in your industry.

Customers change their ordering patterns in tough times. Your phones ring less as customers place fewer orders. They order in smaller quantities and fewer items, ordering only those things necessary for routine maintenance. The average invoice amount decreases. They may substitute low-grade quality for the higher quality products they generally order. They may seek to consolidate purchasing to take advantage of quantity discounts and shipping costs.

As customers experience tough times, they seek ways to stretch their cash. When interest rates go up, money becomes more expensive. Talk to your accounting people and watch accounts receivable. If your accounts currently age at an average of thirty days and that number increases to forty days, tough times are on the horizon.

Similar to changing their ordering habits and paying late, customers ask about cancellation fees and extended terms. When things get tough, financial concerns top the list of customer worries. They pursue all financial options to help them make it through economic downturns.

Price objections in tough times go beyond the normal griping that customers do as part of their negotiating strategy to nibble away at your prices. Your customers are complaining that things are tight, and they are feeling a lot of pressure to economize. Their complaints surface in various ways: slowdown in the market, layoffs, greater competitive pressures, increased demand for maximizing shareholder value, and Wall Street pressure for earnings. Many people believe the current economic downturn is Wall Street induced as CEOs attempt to boost earnings.

One of my clients told me that many of the decisions his top management team made were designed specifically to maximize shareholder value. Since the executive committee making these tough decisions collectively held a substantial number of stock options, it raised suspicion among the rank and file that the measures they had taken were designed to benefit the management team. True or not, you cannot lead employees out of tough times if they suspect you are acting out of self interest.

You may begin to notice competition from companies that never crossed your path in the past. They may be coming from other areas of the country or even over the Internet. Their prices are lower, and they promise customers they will provide services equal to your bundle of value. These may be companies that are diversifying and getting into your business as a way to keep their doors open, or they may just be other regional companies trying to skim whatever easy business they can retrieve with cheaper prices. This may allow them to sell more profitably in their areas while ruining your marketplace.

The media loves to report bad news, and anything that smacks of negativism lights up their radar screens. When the economy is steaming along and someone in the media picks up on some news of economic difficulties, they scramble to scoop the story. Bad news about consumer spending habits, housing starts, automotive sales, corporate layoffs, and disappointing earnings make their way to the front page as the next major crisis we face.

Tough times bring out sale ads touting the lowest prices in decades, scores of articles on how to deal with tough times, financial planner interviews on how to manage one's personal finances during economic downturns, news stories about the bears running wild on Wall Street, cynics being interviewed everywhere, talking heads interviewing academics, and politicians spoon feeding their solutions to their constituents.

Everyone knows someone who is negative—the Chicken Little of economic doom and gloom. But tough times show up in various places. Charities report that donations are down, you find it easier to get a tee time on the golf course during the week, the UPS driver tells you that his deliveries are down, you go to an auto dealer and five salespeople descend on you like you're the last red-hot lead in their business, or you visit the local Harley-Davidson dealer and you can actually buy a Harley off the showroom floor and negotiate price. You travel to Chicago and do not have to stand in line for a taxi cab. Real estate is cheap, leasing rates are even cheaper, and everyone you know who owns a boat is selling it and thinking about dumping their lake home. Business people begin to wear their suits again and shine their shoes, as they search for new opportunities. You can park closer to mall entrances because fewer people are shopping, and the retailers are singing the blues.

Being aware of tough times signals does not mean that you are creating the self-fulfilling prophecy. Some argue that ignorance is bliss; I would counter with Sir Francis Bacon's quote, "Knowledge is power."

> ➤ Being aware of what happens around you, remaining vigilant, and listening to your customers eliminates the element of surprise when tough times hit.

You're prepared because you knew it could happen. Your preparation will serve you well. As others waste time trying to figure out what has happened, you pursue the opportunities in your market.

Three biggest mistakes salespeople make in tough times

Based on years of research, we've identified the biggest and costliest mistakes that salespeople make in tough times and tough markets. Understanding these mistakes will give you an edge in your market.

1. They reduce face-to-face calling by 38%.

According to a purchasing management study, during tough times, salespeople call on customers at 62% the rate they call on customers during good economic times. One can only assume the reasons for this. They may feel that no one is buying and that it makes little sense to call on buyers when things are tough. Salespeople may reduce calling to avoid rejection and price resistance. Some salespeople may call less frequently because they don't know what to talk about in tough times—they've run out of ammunition and hope. They may reduce calling because their companies have redirected their sales efforts elsewhere. A customer told me that his sales force's greatest challenge in time management is how to balance collections in tough times with selling activities. "It's hard to make a sales call and a collections call on the same visit," my client said.

For whatever reason, salespeople cut their face time with customers significantly in tough times. The remedy is to increase your calling by 25%. If you call on customers at a rate of 125% of the rate you normally call, and your competition calls at a rate of 62% of the rate they normally call, you have effectively doubled your coverage! You're calling at twice the rate of the competition.

2. *Salespeople believe everything customers tell them and allow it to bias their presentations.*

If you call on four customers and all of them tell you how tough things are, you may erroneously assume that it's that tough for everyone. This may bias your next presentation. For example, you may say this to the buyer, "Mr. Buyer, I understand from many of our other customers that the market is soft now. Are things as tough for you as they are for everyone else?" If this customer has an ounce of horse trader in him, he will elaborate on how his business is suffering and how desperately he needs relief from your higher prices. Just as some sellers prevail in tough times, some customers prevail in tough times.

> ➤ Never assume that because some customers are suffering, all are suffering.

You may create your own misery with a customer if you give him or her the opportunity to wield bad news for negotiating advantage.

3. Salespeople cut price versus sell value.

This is always the easiest way to resolve price objections, but generally the costliest way for sellers to handle them in tough times. When you cut the price, say good-bye to your margins because it's doubtful they will increase when tough times are over. Ninety percent of salespeople offer a cheaper price unprompted to get the business. We surveyed purchasing agents and discovered that 75% of salespeople cave in when the buyer objects to their prices. And only 18% of salespeople ever close without discounting. Our studies further identified that buyers want their costs cut during tough times. Many salespeople interpret this as *price* cutting. If one out of six shoppers is a price shopper, one out of six salespeople is a price seller. These salespeople rely on price to do the heavy lifting for them.

> ➢ At the heart of most price resistance is a perceived lack of equity. Buyers want to feel they are getting as good as they are giving.

Put your emphasis on building the buyer's perception of your value. If you rely heavily on price to salvage the business, you may regret the business that it salvages. It may be salvage-yard business.

Seven things buyers worry about in tough times

It's not just sellers who fret in tough times, buyers worry, too. This is what your customers worry about in tough times:

1. Financial concerns

Buyers rank money at the top of their worry list in tough times: terms, budgets, and cash flow. As corporate executives seek ways to grow their bottom lines, they slash budgets, cut costs, and hammer suppliers for cheaper prices. Buyers may ask for extended terms, especially if interest rates are high. It's cheaper to borrow money from suppliers than from banks. Banks get stingy in tough times. They like to hoard their money when it's scarce. In fact, one of the harbingers of tough times is that fewer bankers call on me when the economy slows.

Small companies live and die by cash flow. "Do we have enough money coming in to match the money going out?"

This is a common question small business owners ask their accounting managers. Balancing cash flow, receivables and payables, is a daily reality for small businesses. Cash flow is the lifeblood of these organizations. Imagine the competitive advantage of a small company that has substantial cash reserves and can take advantage of buying opportunities in tough times. Fortunes are made during tough times, as forward-thinking business owners take advantage of the buying opportunities. They are perched for the economy to shift, and they compete at a higher level with their investments in new technology, employees, and efficiencies.

2. Cost containment

Buyers want lower costs, not just cheaper prices. In tough times, their overall concern with costs surfaces as a price objection, but it is really more of a concern with lower operating costs. The National Association of Purchasing Managers recently surveyed purchasing agents and found that 75% of them believe technology will help them achieve their efficiency goals.

> ➢ Demonstrate how your technology fits into their efficiency plans. Frame your product in its best cost-cutting light.

Reframe price objections as questions about cost containment. For example, "Are you asking how we can help you increase your efficiency and profit on this project?"

If you sell a time-saving device, and if the customer has few internal resources to do the work, your strongest benefit may be the time you give buyers. You're giving them more of what they have little of—time. They are able to redeploy these resources in other areas. This is the premise behind outsourcing—a favorite in tough times. Companies prefer outsourcing in tough times because it's cheaper to bring in contract labor for specific projects. When the project is complete, the overhead costs leave with the contract employees.

3. Clear buying priorities

In tough times, buyers require a clearer sense of needs versus wants. *Needs* are mission critical. These are things they must do and things they must have in order to accomplish their goals. If you sell needs-oriented solutions, they must have your product. *Wants* are things the buyer would like to have. Selling to the buyer's wants in tough times is more challenging. Here's the seller's paradox: Buyers are more price-sensitive for *needs* and less price-sensitive for *wants*. When was the last time you heard someone complain about the price of a new Mercedes Benz, Rolex, or Mont Blanc pen? Buyers complain about the cost of energy, milk, and healthcare—the necessities in life.

4. Market conditions

Buyers worry if they will be able to compete profitably for their customers' business. This is one of the critical drivers of price resistance in tough times. Your customers interpret their customers' request for cheaper prices as the way to compete in their industries. As an outsider, I might ask the question, "Are they really asking you for a cheaper price so they may compete better, or are they asking for help when competing in a price-sensitive market?" Never assume your price is too high; maybe their expectations are too low, or the competition is desperate to sell.

5. Employee issues

In tough times, companies lay off employees. This hurts morale and feeds a general insecurity in workers. In addition to layoffs, companies cut costs, which includes salaries and vital resources employees need to perform their jobs adequately. This, too, leads to morale problems. Most people want to do good work and get discouraged when the tools and equipment they have to work with do not equal their motivation to perform at their peaks.

Another concern for companies is brain drain, as more talented employees seek stability in other companies or industries. Creative and talented employees get frustrated when they see their ideas put on hold or shelved during tough times.

> ➤ Retaining these innovative employees is as important to an organization as retaining key customers. These employees will help their companies think their way out of tough times.

When companies lay off talented workers during tough times, it's doubtful that they will be able to rehire them when tough times subside. A friend of mine told me about his need to cut costs by the equivalent of one salary per month. The problem he faces is that the short-term—the $2,000 per month he saves from wages—is overshadowed by the training costs of a new person when tough times are over. He decided to bite the bullet and keep the employee— a good long-range decision on his part. He will also save himself the headache, the time, and the expense of finding and training the right person down the road.

One of my clients, who is experiencing tough times just like the rest of us, is using tough times to hire a couple of high-caliber rookie salespeople. Because they are seeking employment, he sees tough times as an opportunity to snag great talent. He is preparing for the future. He will have talented, seasoned, and trained salespeople in place when the economic spigot opens. Guess who benefits long-range from this? His company, of course. While other companies are selecting and training new people, his sales force— already trained—will be out there writing orders.

6. Facilities

Many companies must upgrade or replace equipment, but they do not have the resources to do it. They know the timing is perfect to buy, but their lack of resources holds them back. They are missing a buying opportunity that could position them for success after the storm passes. This is the equivalent to a great buying opportunity for an undervalued stock. It's a blue-chip, traditional, stable company that is currently selling at its one-year low. In the next year, it will most likely double its value. You would love to purchase several thousand shares but have no discretionary money to buy the stock. History has proven your instincts about stocks, but you still lack the resources to take advantage of this buying opportunity. This is how frustrating it can be for your customers if they know they must upgrade, see a buying opportunity, but lack the resources to move forward.

> ➤ The best time to upgrade is when the economy is slow and suppliers and service providers are hungry. Unfortunately, those who need it the most, often have the fewest resources to invest.

This is similar to how farmers deal with winter. They use winter to work on equipment and prepare for the "spring of hope." They prepare for the winter; they know it will come. Too many managers fail to prepare for tough times because they delude themselves into believing that their euphoria will last forever. Economic nirvana is always followed by economic nervousness, which is always followed by economic nirvana. The best time to prepare for tough times is during good times. Peter Drucker said that one of the three biggest problems American managers have is their short-term, quarter-to-quarter mentality.

7. *General anxiety*

The seventh thing on customers' minds in tough times is the same thing that plagues everyone else: a generalized sense of anxiety or fear, as they see their 401Ks slipping, their margins shrinking, and their customers leaving. It takes a special person, buyer or seller, to face tough times bravely and not allow it to affect their attitude.

> ➢ The same things that bother you in tough times also bother your customers.

Empathy and understanding go a long way in helping you help them. People need reassurance and acceptance when they feel anxious. They want to know that things will be okay again, that they're okay, and that they are not alone in their fight.

What buyers really want

We invest heavily in tracking buyer trends and desires. Every year we survey thousands of purchasers to determine what is most important to them. For example, we know that industrial buyers rely more on distributors now than they did five years ago.

> ➢ Customers prefer the manufacturer's cheaper prices, but they want the distributor's service.

On a broader scale, they are saying that price is important, but service is more important. Battles are won with logistics. Distributors are the logistics arms of most manufacturers. Seventy-eight percent of buyers say they use the value added that these companies provide and will not shop price if they are convinced that the value added is in place. Seventy-two percent of buyers say they will not shop price if they are convinced that the supplier is offering genuine, not perceived, value added. Sixty-two percent of buyers say they are pushing their suppliers to increase their overall value to the buyer.

Here are the top ten things that buyers want from sellers:

1. Knowledgeable salespeople

This has been the most stable buyer preference over the years. It has ranked consistently number one since we began surveying buyer preferences. Customers want to deal with knowledgeable salespeople who understand the customer's business and can prescribe the right solution for their problems. Seventy-six percent of the value added in North America comes from knowledge-based activities.

2. Product or service quality

The concern for quality and value skyrockets in tough times. With limited resources to spend, buyers want great value for their money. Buyers are addicted to quality. Your prescription is to feed their addictive beast. Quality is the single most important product feature you offer in tough times. The problem most companies have is that everyone in their industry sells good quality. The quality movement took care of that. Buyers use quality as first-cut criteria and exclude any supplier that offers inferior quality.

3. Product or service availability

Buyers want their supplies or services when they need them—sooner versus later. "Can I get what I need from you when I need it?" This is the question that runs through most buyers' minds when they evaluate your package. The cheapest price in the world is meaningless if the quality is inferior, and the buyer cannot get the product. Which do you think keeps a buyer awake at night, paying more than they anticipated or not having the products they need when they need them to do the job they must do?

4. Ease of doing business

How easy is your company to do business with? Do you make it easy for the customer to purchase your solution? Are your policies flexible enough to accommodate unique buyer problems? Flexibility and adaptability enable you to thrive in tough times. Buyers view your ease of doing business as a measure of your company's management philosophy. Inflexible policies signal inflexible management. Flexibility in implementing company policies and procedures mirrors flexibility in management. If you were the buyer, from whom would you rather buy, a flexible company that is willing to accommodate customer's special needs or a seller that expects the customer to adapt to the seller's way of doing business?

5. *Technical support*

Anyone who has purchased a new computer or any other technical device and needed support service understands the importance of this buyer preference. This includes how long the buyer remains on hold when they call for technical support. A salesperson in one of my seminars told me how one of his competitors lost a large customer because whenever the buyer called for technical support, the supplier put him on hold for an average of twenty-two minutes! How would you deal with this loss of business if this were your account?

I purchased a well-known, branded phone system for our training center. I had some technical questions and called their technical support help line. It took me eight submenus to get to "hold." Ironically, the technology they promote as a more efficient way to route calls is also the most effective way to alienate customers. As I have tracked the performance of this company over the past three years, it's no surprise they are on a downward spiral from which they may not recover. High-tech does not replace high-touch. Buying and selling is still a relationship business.

6. *Acquisition price*

This is the highest ranking that price has ever appeared in our research, and you may conclude that price is now more important than ever. It is number six now because we factored in several thousand automotive and heavy-duty truck buyers' responses to reflect preferences across the board. When we split cost into acquisition price and usage cost, usage cost displaces acquisition price as the buyers' financial priority. Buyers want cost containment over price cuts. Cutting your price is only one of many ways to help your buyers achieve their profit improvement goals. Get creative, and protect your margins.

7. Ability to get things done

As a salesperson, how effectively do you perform your job? Can you create the results your customers want and need? One study found that salesperson competence was the number one factor accounting for buyer satisfaction. Buyers want results and expect you to create them. This includes internal selling inside your organization to create the results that your buyer desires. The folks you deal with on the inside of your company are internal customers. How you work with them determines how well your company performs for the customer. I've never met a good "external" salesperson who wasn't a great "internal" salesperson.

8. Follow up on promises

Do you deliver on your promises? When asked what irritated them most about salespeople, buyers said their top gripe was salespeople not following up on promises. You must follow this practice: Promise a lot, but deliver more. This includes: on-time performance, sending literature, arranging for samples, routine post-sale visits, and timely quotes. A salesperson's word and reputation are more valuable than a cheap price.

9. Product performance

This item prompts a lot of discussion in our seminars because it sounds like product quality. The natural assumption is that quality products perform well. Buyers perceive a difference and want proof that your product will perform at levels that make a difference for the customer, whether it's cutting costs, saving time, or delivering better results. Perceived value is different than performance value. Perceived value excites buyers; performance value satisfies buyers. Perceived value is qualitative and performance value is quantitative. Buyers want perceived value, but they need performance value.

10. Support after the sale

Will you be there for the customer after they have paid for your goods and services? In value added selling, we call this defensive selling—the sale after the sale.

> ➢ Do you treat your customers as if they were prospects? They are, for the competition. Are you working as hard to keep your customers as you did to get them? Am I better off being your prospect or your customer?

Your message should not change in tough times. Stay the course. Continue to sell your company's value added solution and customize your message to these buyer preferences. Stability is one of your great strengths in tough times. Buyers draw security from knowing that they are dealing with a company that is confident enough in their package that they can weather any storm. Be their beacon to help guide them through the economic storm.

Buyers want quality products at "mach one" response time—the speed of sound. They want to contain and control their costs; price is only a small part of cost. They want technical support and innovation. Your job is to demonstrate how your solution adds value to their situation. In tough times especially, your value added must be the real thing, not a marketing cliché. Explain and document your value added for the customer. Make it easy for them to justify the investment, not expense, in tough times.

> ➢ Your solution must help them pull their way
> out of tough times, not push them deeper
> into tough times.

"Mr. Buyer, there are things that help you rise above tough times and things that push you deeper into tough times. Our solution is part of the magic that will help you emerge victorious from tough times." This must be your daily message. Never lose sight of your company's ability to make a difference for the customer. You're in this for the long-haul, good or bad times.

Competitive realities of tough times

Selling and managing successfully in tough times is not a Pollyanna-ish experience. You face tough realities when things slow down.

1. Panic

Seventy percent of today's CEOs have never led a company out of tough times. Sixty percent of salespeople have never sold in a recession. We have a generation of lower level managers who have never managed a sales force in tough times leading salespeople who were not in sales during the recession of 1990-91. We have experienced salespeople who have just come off a ten-year winning streak who are trying to remember what it's like to sell in tough times.

Most people panic in tough times—buyers, sellers, your management, your competition, your peers, and maybe you. Weak competitors and frightened customers are a bad combination for companies that want to compete on a higher level. Desperate people do desperate things. Know that your best customer may bounce you in tough times if they feel it's in their best interest. Be prepared for this. Be proactive. Reassure them. Help them deal with their panic.

2. Price cutting

When weaker competitors desperately begin cutting their prices, don't compound their ignorance with your own. "If all of the other kids in the neighborhood jumped in the lake, would you follow?" When your parents admonished you as a child, they were preparing you for selling in tough times. You must remain steady and committed to protecting your margins. The problem with cutting your prices in tough times is that you are giving away the resources you need for competitive advantage—profit. Are you cutting your price or cutting your throat? Weak competitors will implement self-defeating strategies because they are desperate. In this case, you are better advised to take Napoleon's advice, "Never interrupt an enemy when he is making a mistake."

➢ Buyers test your price, then they test your resolve.

3. Fighting on the wrong battlefield

In the movie, *Gettysburg*, the generals paid close attention to the ground they chose to fight the battle. One of the memorable lines from the movie is, "This is lovely ground for fighting." They knew to prevail, they must choose the right ground—the high ground for battle.

Choose your battleground, not the competition's battleground. If price is not your strength, don't fight a price battle. You cannot out-Wal-Mart a Wal-Mart when it comes to price. Choose to fight where you are strong. If your strength is speed, stay with it. Sell it. If your strength is quality, stay on message. Concentrate on your message of quality and support in tough times. Be stubborn in presenting your message consistently. Choose your strategy, not your competitor's strategy.

4. No money

The business world can be a cold place to work; it is numbers driven. You cannot make someone buy if they have no money. You can't even make someone buy if they have money. But you can make them wish they had the money to spend with you or encourage them to put you at the top of their priorities list when times get better. In Chapter 3 of this book, I offer some ideas for how you can dig for discretionary dollars.

One of my customers told me recently that his sales for repair items are off because the maintenance people in the plants have discovered that the only way to get money for new equipment is if they need to replace the entire system. These maintenance employees let the equipment break down because their companies have decided that replacement is the only acceptable expenditure.

5. It's a demand issue

What you're experiencing is a buying problem, not a selling problem. Are your skills any worse in tough times?

They may be rusty, but they will get better quickly. Do you know less about your product in tough times? Is your solution worth less in tough times? No. No. No. The problem is that the buyer is not buying—you're still selling! You may not be selling all that you would like to be selling, but you *are* selling—they're just not buying. You're continuing to do your job, even though you may be frustrated. You can't take that to the bank, but you are controlling what you can control—your input. Continue to focus on selling, and quit listening to the bad news bears. Their job is to report the negative stuff; your job is to move forward. Someone must be in the 5% who thrive in tough times; it might as well be you.

Summary

Tough times exist. If you're in sales and management long enough, you will experience tough times. Tough times exist when you're working harder and harder to stay where you are. Regardless of the industry, most salespeople believe they sell in tough markets. Salespeople make three major mistakes in tough times: they reduce face time with customers, believe everything they hear, and cut their prices. Buyers, like sellers, worry in tough times about the economy, how to compete successfully in their markets, employee issues, financial problems, and general anxiety. Buyers want more than a cheap price; they want quality, availability, performance, follow-up, a fair price, technical support, knowledgeable salespeople, ease of doing business, delivery on promises, and service after the sale. In tough times, people panic—customers, competitors, and maybe your peers. Your mission is to remain focused and stay the course.

2

The Tough Times Attitude

*Nothing can stop the man with the right mental attitude
from achieving his goal; nothing on earth
can help the man with the wrong mental attitude.*
Thomas Jefferson, Third President of the United States

Do you have the right mental attitude or the wrong mental attitude? Half the battle is in your head; the other half is on the streets. Or, as that great American philosopher, Yogi Berra, said, "Ninety percent of the game is half mental." In this chapter, I focus on the mental side of selling and managing in tough times and tough markets. You will find that many of the ideas in this section will help you in other areas of your life where you face adversity. I share with you some positive and negative attitudes I've heard from salespeople over the years and a dozen ways to program yourself mentally for success. Seven years of professional study in psychology, twenty-plus years of motivational training, and a few bumps in the road along the way have provided me with a practical and theoretical foundation for this information.

Attitude and behavior

We move in the direction of our thoughts; we become what we think about. Years ago I purchased a Stearman biplane and flew it from New Hampshire to St. Louis. I asked a friend to accompany me as my navigator and copilot. I flew, he watched. Somewhere over the mountains of western New York state, he yelled into the Stearman's primitive intercom, "Are you looking left?"

I yelled back, "Yeah."

We flew another ten minutes, and he asked, "Are you looking right?"

Again I replied, "Yeah."

After another ten minute leg he asked, "Are you looking left?"

I responded, "Yes. Why do you keep asking me that question?"

He said, "The way you look, we fly in that direction."

We flew my line of sight. If I looked left, I unwittingly moved the stick left; the airplane followed. If I looked right, my hand followed the line of sight, and we flew right, off course.

> ➤ We move in the direction of our thoughts. We become what we think about.

This is the foundation for the self-fulfilling prophecy. Our beliefs set in motion activities creating results that confirm our expectations.

Attitude drives behavior. We behave as we believe. We follow our beliefs, and the outcome of the behavior reinforces our beliefs. It's self-reinforcing. This works for both positive and negative beliefs. If you begin a task by believing that you will succeed, you have a greater probability of succeeding than if you begin with a negative expectation of the outcome.

Perception is the meaning you attach to incoming stimuli. Your meaning is often linked to your attitudes and beliefs. That's why two people can see the same event and interpret it differently. It's the glass-is-half-filled/half-empty debate. For the optimist, it's half full. For the pessimist, it's always half-empty, even if he has just filled it half-way.

As the thirty-third President of the United States, Harry Truman faced a monumental decision to end World War II. Most of us never experience tough times that remotely compare with his situation. He maintained his positive focus in dark times: "A pessimist is someone who makes difficulties of his opportunities; an optimist is one who makes opportunities of his difficulties."

James Allen wrote, "The good or the bad is not in the circumstance, but only in the mind of him that encounters it." And William Shakespeare said, "There is nothing either good or bad, but thinking makes it so." Implicit in these thoughts is the reality that *we have a choice for how we perceive the world we live in.*

What do you see in this illustration?

Some people look at this illustration and see the chalice; others see two opposing faces. Psychologists use this to demonstrate perception to students. The practical value for us in business is that there is always more than one way to view something. We all see that same image but interpret it differently. Our interpretation depends on our frame of reference, life experiences, and our expectations.

Behaviors repeated over time become habits. Everyone has habits—good, bad, or neutral. The key to effectively navigating rough waters is to have more good habits than bad habits. By practicing the behavioral side of *How to Sell and Manage in Tough Times and Tough Markets*, you develop habits that will serve you well. For most salespeople, it becomes habit substitution versus radical changes in behavior. You currently have a time management habit. In tough times, you may need to set priorities differently. You're still setting priorities, but you may decide something's importance by different standards in tough times.

Everyone is motivated. Some are motivated to rise to the challenge in tough times; others are motivated to avoid tough times. How you perceive tough times and your confidence in your ability to make a difference will determine your behavior and your success in tough times. Even negative salespeople are motivated; they're just motivated to say and do negative things.

Negative salespeople attract negative attention. According to one management study, cynics are the first ones to be shuffled out of a company in tough times. Who needs negative people around when things are already tough? Managers perceive them as a cancer that eats away at the collective psyche of the sales force.

> ➢ When you're negative, the only people you attract are other negative people.

Fredrich Nietzsche, a nineteenth-century German philosopher, said, "When I stare into the abyss, it stares back at me." They like your negativism because it makes them feel better about their problems. Some are even thrilled that you have negative things going on in your life. In a twisted, low self-esteem sort of way, they feel validated by it. The German word "schadenfreude" describes this phenomenon when one person takes pleasure in the misery of others.

Right and wrong thoughts for tough times

Here is a sample of negative attitudes I've heard from salespeople about tough times and tough markets:

- Price is the only thing that sells in our industry.
- The only thing buyers care about is a cheap price.
- The only way to compete in our market is to have the absolute lowest price.
- Our industry is all bid.
- There are no more negotiated deals out there.
- I've got everybody's price shopper in my territory.
- It's a waste of time to convince someone to pay more for something.
- Forget service and support, the only thing that really counts is a cheap price.
- Hey, if I don't cut the price I'll lose the business.
- I shop price, doesn't everyone?
- What I sell is no different than anybody else. It's the same. There isn't a dime's worth of difference between my product and the competition.

- It's out of my hands. I'm helpless in the process.
- Heck, I'd feel guilty selling at that price. It's gouging the customer.
- It takes too much effort to avoid price objections.
- You can't sell in tough times or tough markets.
- It's different in my industry.

Imagine the impact this attitude has on the salesperson's behavior—they are defeated before they start. Contrast these negative attitudes with the following list of positive attitudes for tough times:

- There are buyers who will pay more for a better solution. I've witnessed this in the past. I've seen these buyers. I've sold to them. I know who they are.
- Price is only one of several variables that go into the decision process. There are many things that affect the buyer's decision to buy.
- My attitude about price affects my profit margins and my success.
- We sell something special, and I'm excited about what we can do for the buyer.
- No product is overpriced unless the customer under-desires it.
- My success in tough times stems directly from my preparation and my attitude.
- The more value I build in on the front end, the less important price becomes on the back end.

- The more I study our product and service, the more passionate I become about them. This passion fuels my conviction. And it is this conviction that makes me persuasive.
- If I have 20% market share, that means I have an 80% opportunity share to pursue.

As you study this list of negative and positive attitudes, which describes your attitude more accurately? If the list of negative thoughts reflects your beliefs, you need to give yourself a mental enema to abandon this thinking. Your behavior will never change as long as you harbor these beliefs. If you sound more like the positive list, keep up the great work!

- Pessimists see problems; optimists see challenges.
- Pessimists see adversity as a never-ending phenomenon; optimists see adversity as temporary delays.
- Pessimists see their problems raging out of control; optimists compartmentalize their adversity.
- Pessimists feel helpless; optimists feel hopeful.
- Pessimists put their heads down and run for cover; optimists hold their heads up and plow another row.

Characteristics of tough timers

Have you ever noticed that some people confront tough times head-on and continue to pursue their goals? They won't quit. Quitting is not an option. They get up every morning, lick their wounds, dress for battle, and fight the good fight. You see them in all walks of life, not just sales. Whether they are business people, professional athletes, or social workers, these tough timers share common denominators that serve as a benchmark for the rest of us.

1. Courage

Winston Churchill said, "Courage is the first of human qualities because it is the quality which guarantees all other qualities." Everything else emanates from your willingness to face adversity head-on. Human beings are hard-wired to detect adversity. It is part of the survival instinct. We sense danger and lock in quickly on threatening events.

Someone once defined courage as "fear that has said its prayers." Ernest Hemmingway defined courage as "grace under pressure." I spent four years in the United States Army from 1969 to 1973. As we prepared for war, they taught us that courage was "the management of fear, not the absence of fear."

Tough timers have courage. They make the tough calls and do the right thing. They never consider quitting as a viable option. It requires courage to fight a battle that you know you could lose. It takes courage to face your greatest fear. It takes courage to thrive in tough times. It takes greater courage to pursue something when you risk failure than to chase a sure thing. When you meet someone who has prevailed in tough times, the first thing you notice is a serenity that reflects their courage.

2. Limited focus

Those who thrive in good times or tough times focus with laser-like intensity on those things that will give them the return they desire. Focus is positive tunnel vision. In good times, it means locking in on your goals and pursuing them with enthusiasm and determination. In tough times, it means locking in your goals and locking out the distractions along the way.

When tough timers face adversity, they limit the reach and the scope of the problem. They do not generalize the event so that it consumes their entire lives. They focus on the immediate impact area of the adversity. Imagine the impact of letting adversity run amuck in your mind. The problem rages, as an out-of-control forest fire, leaving thousands of acres of mental ashes. You cannot focus on the solution because the problem is too far reaching. Compartmentalizing the adversity helps tough timers focus narrowly on a workable solution. Losing a sale is not the end of someone's life. It's not even close. A lost sale is only a lost sale. You probably will not lose your job if you lose a sale. Your life will not end if you lose a sale. Your company will not go out of business if you lose a single sale. Your career is not over if you lose a single sale.

> ➤ Tough timers compartmentalize their adversity and limit its reach.

Be clear on what I'm saying. I don't want you feeling too good about losing a sale, but a good mental conversation to have with yourself is to isolate the adversity to the one specific area of your life that it directly impacts. Your family will still love you, even if you lose the sale. Your best friend will still be your best friend tomorrow, if you happen to lose the sale. To prevail in tough times, remind yourself that you're dealing with a specific form of adversity that will not ripple into every other aspect of your life, leaving catastrophe after catastrophe in its wake.

3. Perceived control

Tough timers view adversity from a position of control. They understand life in terms of things they control and things they cannot control. This paradoxical blend of seizing and yielding builds their confidence for dealing with tough times. They view tough circumstances and ask themselves, "What *can* I control in this situation?" They may discover that the only thing they *can* control is their own reaction to the situation. It's impossible to manage a tough situation, which may be spiraling out of control, when you're caught in a whirlpool of your own emotions. Focus on what you can control in adversity: your emotions and your actions.

Self-discipline and control go hand in hand. When you're clear on what you control, it's easier to exercise a disciplined response. Adversity is chaos. When you respond to chaos with your own version of chaos—an undisciplined reaction—you add to the confusion of the situation. To bring order to chaos, you must exercise control and discipline over that which you have the most control—yourself and your reaction.

4. Problem ownership

Tough timers feel responsible for taking action regardless of the cause of the adversity or whose problem it is. In a street-smart way, they feel they can make a difference with their input. This is not a neurotic feeling of unbridled accountability for all of the misery in the world. I'm referring to someone who confronts adversity head-on and says to himself or herself, "I can do something about this." They would rather fix the problem than fix the blame. They prefer to take action instead of taking cover.

> ➤ Tough timers fix the problem, not the blame.

Years ago I spoke at a meeting, and the video company mistakenly brought the wrong equipment for my presentation. The vice president that hired me could see the difficulties we were having and asked about the problem. His next question redirected the crisis to the solution, "What do we need to do to fix it?" He had no interest in fixing the blame; he wanted to fix the problem.

5. Creativity

Tough timers always see a way out of difficulty. Creativity is fundamental to resilience and persistence. To become more creative you must learn how to think out of the box. Approach the problem differently. For example, I was helping my son deal with a small "catastrophe" in his summer painting business. He needed to start his painting job on a certain date. As he got closer to the date, he did not have all of his equipment ready for the job, and panic set in. Specifically, he didn't have a way to transport his 32-foot extension ladder to the job site; his construction trailer was being outfitted.

We were driving to the hardware store to pick up some supplies, and an SUV passed us with a canoe secured to the roof of the vehicle. I noticed how it was attached, and it gave me an idea how we could attach his ladder to my brand new SUV, which I had been reluctant to do earlier. Being open to different ideas allowed us to creatively attach his ladder and meet the deadline. Trust your creativity. Encourage your creativity. Feed your creativity.

6. Perseverance

Tough timers persist until they win. They know nothing great was ever accomplished by a quitter. They persist because they embrace the attitude, "This, too, will pass." They know, at a gut-level, there is a time limit on tough times. Every downturn in our economy was followed by a period of expansion. Every missed sale is followed by a sale that you make at some point. Knowing that misery will not last fuels tough timers with the hope they need to get up another day and fight the battle.

> ➢ *Victory belongs to the most persevering.*

Napoleon

Three out of four salespeople quit the first time the buyer says, "No." Another 5% quit on the second "No." If you persist beyond the second "No," you will have eliminated 80% of your competition—the quitters. In winning, tough timers discover *there is no traffic jam on the extra mile!*

If you stand on the river bank and watch the water flow over rocks and stumps and sometimes the banks, it is the stones that wear down, not the water. The stones tumble and roll and come to rest as the water continues to flow persistently over the rocks. Salespeople who persist in tough times are like streams and rivers that flow over and around obstacles that may slow them down, but don't stop them. Tough timers turn and twist and flow over obstacles, but rarely quit.

7. Optimism

Tough timers are positive thinkers, but their optimism cuts deeper than happy thoughts. They draw from a well-spring of confidence and hope. Because of their sense of control and creativity, tough timers look at the future through the eyes of an optimist. This is a bone-deep belief in their right and ability to live a positive life. This belief gains traction in positive behaviors. They behave as they believe, and their behavior reinforces their positive beliefs.

Tiger Woods appeared on Oprah after winning his first Master's tournament. Oprah commented on how far he hits the ball and that there was talk the PGA may move the tees back to make it more difficult for him. She asked him, "Does that bother you that they are trying to make it more difficult for you?" With his typical confidence and humility, Tiger replied, "No, because it will be that much tougher for the rest of the players also."

Optimists know tough times affect everyone, but not everyone engages tough times the same way. Some thrive, others fail. Your attitude toward tough times will be your most powerful ally or your most debilitating adversary.

Researchers have studied optimism extensively and found that optimistic salespeople outsell their negative counterparts by a huge margin. If you were to split a sales force in half and compare the sales of the optimistic half to the pessimistic half, you would find that the optimists sell on average 37% more product than their negative counterparts. Martin Seligman, who wrote *Learned Optimism*, found that the top 10% of optimists outsell the bottom 10%—the cynics—by 88%!

Optimists are risk-takers who use their creativity to discover innovative solutions to their problems. They live longer, healthier lives, and suffer fewer depressions than pessimists. They persevere because they feel they can make a difference with their actions.

8. Humor

Humor is one of the best anecdotes for being down in the dumps. In addition to the obvious benefit of laughter, there is a physiological advantage when your brain releases endorphins during laughter. Humor allows you to see the lighter side of adversity. Plato wrote, "Even the gods love jokes."

Abraham Lincoln relied heavily on his sense of humor to deal with the stress he faced as president. He often shared his sense of humor with others to take the edge off a situation. He said, "I laugh because I must not weep—that's all, that's all." When someone commented on Grant's reputation for drinking whiskey, Lincoln responded by suggesting they order barrels of it for the other generals if it would help them create the same results Grant got.

After the Great Flood of '93 engulfed my training center, I sent a letter to my customers advising them how we were doing. I chose humor . . .

Dear Customers:

As many of you no doubt have heard, we have experienced a little water problem in our building in Chesterfield Valley. But don't worry; we're okay—most of our assets are now liquid; cash flow means a little something different to us now; we're swamped but staying afloat and keeping our heads above water. If you want to help, call 1-800-BUY-TAPES!

I continued with our intention to rebuild and start anew. We received many letters and phone calls from concerned customers, but one stands out in my mind. One customer sent me a note saying that he was so impressed by my optimism in the letter that he posted the note in his company's lunch room for all of his employees to read. They loved the puns and embraced the hope.

9. Support group

John Donne, a seventeenth-century English poet and cleric wrote, "No man is an island, entire of itself; every man is a piece of the Continent, a part of the main. . . " This is another way of saying, "We is greater than me." Jack Welch, legendary CEO of G.E., was quoted in the newspaper, "None of us is even close to being as smart as all of us." Who is as strong individually as we are collectively? No one. To prevail in tough times, you need a support group.

When I lost my voice in 1980 to cancer, I was told to get used to the idea that I would probably never talk normally again—my voice was a muted whisper. Fortunately, I had a great support group that included a speech therapist who worked with me three days a week for six months. Our work resulted in a deep, rich baritone voice. The bittersweet irony is that since 1981, I have made a living with my voice. I learned a valuable lesson from this experience. Never let another person tell you what is possible for you. Only you and your Creator know what passion beats in your heart and the full reach of your potential.

Many people believe that the core of your strength is your spiritual dimension. Most religions profess a philosophy of hope for the future. This spiritualism supports and infuses people with the emotional fuel they need to prevail in tough times. For me, I always drew great strength from the words of St. Ignatius Loyola, "Pray as if it all depends on God; work as if it all depends on you." This philosophy encourages us to take initiative while seeking Divine help. Not a bad combination, eh?

> ➢ We is greater than me. You may be able
> to do it on your own, but why would you?

A University of Wisconsin study found that family farmers who rebound from downturns generally have a strong family support unit that bolsters their confidence and offers the support they need to solve the problems they encounter. Families, close friends, and managers make up your support group. Let them help you. You do not have to fight your battle by yourself. Who is your support group?

Positive mental programming

Mental programming is how you talk to yourself, good or bad. Some people call it self-talk. Positive mental programming (PMP) is how to talk to yourself so that you will listen to positive, reinforcing, and inspiring messages. Most people have heard of the computer principle GIGO: garbage in, garbage out. PMP is good in, good out.

Research demonstrates that positive thoughts are important but have a temporary effect in helping people. On the other hand, positive processing is more effective over the long haul for helping people deal effectively with adversity. Positive processing is how you process your world and talk to yourself during success and failure. It's how you attach meaning to the events in your life. By applying the ideas in this section, you will program yourself for success, even in tough times.

1. Dream big dreams

It's okay to dream in tough times. In fact, I recommend it. You do it every night when you close your eyes and fall asleep. Consider this, how did you feel the last time you had a nightmare? Did you awaken with your heart pounding, pulse racing, sweating, crying, shaking, and screaming? Were you too afraid to fall back to sleep? All of this happened in an instant while you were asleep. Imagine what would happen if you were to engage this same dynamic force when you are awake.

When you allow yourself to dream big dreams, your heart thunders in your chest, your blood races through your veins, and you have trouble sleeping at night because you are so excited. There are few things that will lift you as quickly from despair as a great big ol' dream. Dreams spawn hope, which is an important emotional spark for salespeople. Sales is an emotional sport. Do you know what happens if you fail to dream? Nothing.

What if you lived by the question, "What if?" Children do this all the time, but adults seem to lose this *dream-ability*. Children play baseball at Yankee Stadium, fly F-16's, and perform at Carnegie Hall. And they do all of this in their dreams. Robert Schuller challenges us with his question, "What would you attempt if you knew you couldn't fail?" The answer is, "Everything." Set challenging goals that stretch you to your capacity for believing.

Ghandi wrote, "Man often becomes what he believes himself to be. If I keep on saying to myself that I cannot do a certain thing, it is possible that I may end (life) by really becoming incapable of doing it. On the contrary, if I have the belief that I can do it, I shall surely acquire the capacity to do it even if I may not have it at the beginning."

> ➤ It's as if your ability will stretch
> to your capacity for believing.

Dreaming helps you creatively pursue your goals. Many great ideas begin only with the seed of the final product. Creativity and dreaming go hand in glove and enable you to confront adversity with confidence and hope. Dreaming is hope in fast-forward. It's creating the future in your mind, in the present. Many people get trapped in time. They lock in on the past, depriving themselves of the joy of today, and the hope of tomorrow. Dreaming pulls you out of this trap.

Your best antidote to being down in the dumps is to dream something big enough to make your bones itch. If your dream isn't this big, go back to the drawing board and dream bigger. The only thing that limits you is the edge of your imagination.

2. *Expect buffeting*

Buffeting is the natural energy that accompanies change. Physically, you experience this when you haven't exercised in a while and embark on a fitness program. Your muscles are sore. They are informing you that you're making a change. This happens emotionally also.

When you make a decision to try something new, you are stretching emotionally. This has the same effect on you as stretching your muscles. You feel it. You know you're stretching; it's change. It's all that extra-special energy you feel that some people call anxiety. I call it energy because it's a necessary part of the change process. You need that extra energy to get you to "where you want to be" quicker.

I was speaking in Memphis to a group of six hundred people. Prior to this date, I had only spoken to groups of fifty or sixty. As I stood on stage facing the crowd, I felt the most incredible adrenalin rush I had ever felt as a speaker. And then it dawned on me. When you're in front of six hundred people, you're supposed to feel that kind of energy. You transform it into enthusiasm so that the people in the back row can feel the energy that the audience members in the front row feel. That day marked my first standing ovation as a speaker.

Internal buffeting is an important part of the change process. All that nervous energy you feel because of tough times is a bonus. You can use it to lift yourself from tough times. You can use it to rise above the circumstances surrounding your adversity.

> ➤ Buffeting is part of the "fight or flight" response
> that has helped humans confront adversity
> since the beginning of time. We are hard-wired
> for this.

External buffeting is what you experience outside of yourself. When you change, it affects other people around you. They may be more aware of your change than you think, and it may have the opposite effect on them as it does on you. As you attempt to improve your lot in life, your struggle reminds other people of a different kind of struggle they face. You're swimming upstream, and they may be treading water. You're advancing, and they're not. You're selling products that they're not selling. You're succeeding in tough times, and they're struggling to stay afloat. It's as if someone forgot to tell you that salespeople cannot sell in tough times. Brace yourself—they will.

You may hear a chorus of, "What are you trying to do, get a promotion?" or "Don't you know things are bad right now. Nobody can sell in tough times." or "Slow down. You're making the rest of us look bad." Knowing this could happen and recognizing it when it surfaces will prepare you for the feedback you may get from others as you lift yourself out of tough times.

3. Use selective input

Would you allow someone to back up a garbage truck and unload its contents on your front lawn? Probably not. Yet, people do this all the time emotionally when they spread their negativism as liberally as manure. Be careful of what you choose to hear and believe.

> ➤ No one can change your opinion
> without your permission.

Why would you give a cynic the opportunity and the power to infect you with their thinking? Check the source. How much credibility does this person have? Is it news or noise? If you're listening to someone who is perpetually negative, consider that when processing their comments. Negative people say negative things. It's how they process life. Do you want to drink from the same well of negativism as this person? Beware of those who cloak themselves in the sheep's clothing of pragmatism. "I'm just a realist. I'm a practical person." Do you live in an unreal world? Are your dreams unrealistic? Do you want someone else's insecurities holding you back? No. No. No.

Why would you give someone else veto power over your dreams? They are *your* dreams, not theirs. Of course others will not share your enthusiasm. Share your most intimate dreams with *only* those who can and will help you to get where you want to be. Everyone else's opinion is noise against the chorus of your support group.

Throughout my whole life, and at every turn, I have met people who did not share my confidence or my passion for my dreams. Some would laugh. Others would gently remind me that it was something that couldn't be done, especially by a guy like me. Fortunately, I'm an internal big mouth. My inner voice shouted louder than their collective voices, and I persisted. Success along the way will convince you that the most important voice you will listen to is your own. Consider what might have happened if the following people had listened to the naysayers.

- In 1962, four young musicians auditioned for Decca Records. The executives dismissed them saying, "We don't like their sound. Groups of guitars are on their way out." The Beatles left without a contract.
- John Grisham got forty-five rejections before he sold his first novel. He is one of today's hottest-selling writers.
- Louis L'Amour got 350 rejections before he sold his first book. He has written over one hundred novels since then and sold 200 million copies.
- In 1954, Elvis Presley was fired by the manager of the

Grand Ol' Opry who said, "You ain't goin' nowhere son. You oughta go back to drivin' a truck."

◆ After inventing the telephone, Alexander Graham Bell was told by President Rutherford Hayes, "That's an interesting invention, but who would ever want to use one of them?"

As I'm writing this book, the movie, *Pearl Harbor*, just released. The critics gave it only fair reviews, but public opinion is that it's a blockbuster. I have talked to several people, young and old, who loved the movie. Some rated it in the top five movies they had ever seen. It was a commercial success its first weekend at the box office. It only confirms my opinion of critics: If they had anything worth writing, they would write.

4. Practice emotional equity

Give your adversity an appropriate amount of emotion. Why cry when a simple frown will do the trick? Why put yourself into a psychotic despair when simple disappointment will work? Why let your mind run free among all possible worst outcomes when a handful of insecurities work nicely for the situation? Feel the pain and move on.

> ➤ *There is no education like adversity.*
>
> Benjamin Disraeli

I was talking to a friend one day about the untimely passing of his wife. Of course there's never a good time to lose a loved one. My friend is a therapist who has spent his entire professional life helping people get beyond their present and past circumstances. Now the therapist needed a therapist. I said to him, "What are you going to do now?"

He responded in his typical way of viewing adversity, "I'll tell you what I'm not going to do. I'm not going to travel for six months or pour myself into my career, trying to forget my pain. I'm going home every night to an empty house and cry when I feel the need to cry. I'm going to grieve for the love of my life. And then I will heal."

I stood there speechless. I felt like a mind voyeur as I listened to his self-talk that he so freely shared with me. "I'm going to feel the pain and move on." As my friend continued, I was struck by his clarity in the midst of pain and adversity. He knew what he must do. Grieve and move on.

> ➢ Of course you will feel disappointment when you lose a sale. You worked hard to earn it. Why wouldn't you feel disappointment?

All that macho stuff about it being the customer's loss is baloney. Losing hurts. To paraphrase a great football coach, show me a good loser, and I'll show you a loser. Denial is highly overrated as a defense mechanism. Do you feel good when you work hard to make a sale and accomplish your goal? Sure you do. You will feel disappointment when you fail. You're supposed to feel disappointment. It's a measure of your commitment. Resilience depends on the depth and length of your response. How long and how deeply will you let yourself feel the pain?

My friend's advice rings clearly in the bell tower of my mind: Feel the pain and move on. You've been in tough situations before and rebounded. Short of a life-threatening illness, your life will not end because of the circumstance you're in. Failure, or whatever adversity you face, will not be etched on your headstone. Give your adversity the measured and equitable attention it deserves and move on. Feel the pain, and redirect your energy toward living and pursuing your goals.

5. Seize control.

Locus of control refers to how you perceive control over your life. If you perceive many of the things that happen to you as the result of choices you make and actions you take, you are *internally controlled*. If you perceive much of what happens in your life as the result of forces beyond your control—luck or fate—you are *externally controlled*. Internally controlled people go through life by choice; externally controlled people go through life by chance. Internally controlled people feel victorious in their lives; externally controlled people feel like victims of circumstances. Internally controlled prevail in tough times; externally controlled people struggle in tough times. Most of the things we experience in life are the result of decisions we make and the actions we take.

Here is a list of statements you might hear from someone who is externally controlled:

You have all the luck.

It's not in the cards for me.

I wish I could stop smoking.

You can't sell when the economy is bad.

I'm too young to be successful.

I wish we had a product that sold itself.

If we only had better literature . . .

If I had your territory, I could do as well as you.

Contrast this list with a list of statements you might hear from someone who is internally controlled:

When (not if) I make this happen.

If nothing else, I can control how hard I work.

Luck is where preparation meets opportunity.

Most of what accounts for my success is stuff I control.

The harder I work, the luckier I get.

Ninety percent of what happens to me is the result of my decisions and actions.

If it is to be, it is up to me.

In reality, we're all a little of both. Someone who perceives total control over their life may be unrealistic. Life requires yielding and controlling. A key to successful living is to understand those things over which you exercise control and those things over which you have little or no control. Attend to each with a commensurate amount of energy as you have control.

Invest time and energy in those areas where you have control. Invest little time and energy in those areas where you have little or no control.

You may not be able to control the outcome of a situation, but you can control your reaction and behavior.

At a minimum, you control your input. You cannot control the economy. You cannot even influence it, unless you're the Chairman of the Fed or the President of the United States. However, you can control your reaction to tough economic times. You cannot control your buyer's budget process, but you can control how you approach the buyer. You cannot control your buyer's emotions, but you can control your reaction to the buyer.

When you attend to those areas where you can influence the outcome, you seize control of your destiny. I have an exercise I would like you to try. Make a list of all of those things that will account for success in your career, regardless of the economy or the territory you occupy. I'll give you three examples to prime the pump: quality products, available inventory, and management support. For the next two minutes, brainstorm and write down as many things you can think of that account for your success. Please do not read further until you have completed this exercise. Write them in the book:

Quality products

Available inventory

Management support

_____

_____

_____

_____

_____

_____

_____

_____

_____

_____

_____

_____

_____

_____

_____

_____

_____

Review your list. What appears on it? When I ask sales-people in my seminars to read their lists, this is a sampling of what I hear: attitude, honesty, communication skills, fol-low-up, knowledge, customer focus, enthusiasm, initiative, teamwork, motivation, persistence, time management, and persuasiveness. Do you see a pattern? I ask the salespeople to review their lists and assess how much control they have over any one item. Most of the items on the lists are things over which they have some control—a little or a lot.

> ➤ The message is loud and clear: Focus more on
> those things you control and less on those
> things over which you have little or no control.

You will find that about 90% of the things that account for success in your job are things that you control. The other 10% may require yielding and accepting—going with the flow. That, too, is a valuable skill.

6. Maintain your focus

It is impossible to concentrate on the negative image of a thought. Try not to think of blood running down the pages of this book as you're reading it. If you're sufficient-ly disgusted by this thought, you've proven my point. The more time you invest thinking about what you want to accomplish, the less time you have available obsessing on what you want to avoid.

Focus on goals, not obstacles. Look for opportunities, not barricades. Be thankful for your blessings, don't curse your burdens. To paraphrase an old proverb, you can curse the darkness or light a candle. Focus on the light, not the dark.

> ➤ Concentrate on what you want to achieve, not what you want to avoid.

Remember, we move in the direction of our thoughts. If you obsess on what you want to avoid, you are focusing way too much energy in that direction. You will follow your thoughts and accomplish what you want to avoid. If you find yourself obsessing on negative thoughts or beliefs, use this thought-disruption technique to redirect your thinking:

Step one: Identify the thought or belief.

Step two: Challenge it with these questions.

What is the evidence that this will happen?
Says who?
Why is this belief true?
What is the proof of this belief?

Step three: Is there another way to view this?

Step four: Get busy doing something positive.

For example, you may be obsessing over losing a sale:

Step one: What is the thought?

"I lost an important sale and my boss will fire me."

Step two: Challenge it.

"What is my evidence that this will happen?"

"Has my boss told me that he will fire me if I lose the sale?"

"Has our company ever fired a sales rep for losing one sale?"

Step three: Is there another way to view this?

"My boss will not be happy."

"He may try to encourage me. He has done that in the past."

"I am not the only salesperson who has ever lost a sale."

Step four: Get busy.

"I could begin prospecting for another customer whose business will help compensate for the lost sale."

You will feel disappointed. You should, you worked hard for the business. This thought-disruption exercise will not make the disappointment go away, but it will help you view the situation differently. This results in a more positive conversation with yourself, doesn't it? You're not using denial or any other defense mechanism to ignore the situation. You're arguing a different—and psychologically healthier—point of view.

7. Reinforce the effort

Initially, reinforce the effort, not the results. When you attempt to change behavior, trying is good enough at the start. The key is to get busy. If you haven't made cold calls in a while, you will probably be rough to begin with. Making cold calls is good enough for right now. As you make more calls and gain proficiency, you can begin to shift your attention to the quality of your efforts. You will get better with experience, but trying is good enough to get you moving in the right direction. Too many people are always getting ready to get ready; they procrastinate. Your prescription is to get busy.

Those who complain about how bad things are remind me of the man who put great faith in God but was bemoaning his luck one day because he did not win the big lottery that he prayed hard to win.

He yelled to the heavens, "God, how can You forsake me this way? Don't You command us to trust in You?"

To the man's surprise he heard a booming voice in response, "I'll do My part, but you at least have to buy the ticket if you want to win."

Do something positive about your circumstances. Procrastination never works. When you procrastinate, you avoid acting for whatever reason. The opposite of action is inaction, and nothing happens with inertia.

> ➢ As long as you're initiating action,
> you're not a victim of circumstances.

You're taking control of the situation. Positive action is an important part of confronting tough times. When you feel you're making progress, it reinforces a positive attitude, which continues to drive your behavior. Action is spiritual fuel.

8. Reframe-reprogram-restructure

Viktor Frankl, author-psychiatrist, wrote "the last of human freedoms is . . . (the ability) to choose one's attitude in a given set of circumstances." Choice plays a major role in how you view the world. You choose how you perceive that which happens around you. For example, how do you view the time you spend away from customers? Some people see this downtime as unproductive. If you view it as an opportunity to do something important behind the scenes, how can you consider it unproductive? When customers call to complain, do you view this as an irritation or an opportunity to deliver on your promise of better service?

You can back away from any circumstance and ask yourself these questions, "Is there another way to view this situation?" "Can I interpret this differently?" "Would someone else see the opportunity in this adversity?" There is always more than one way to interpret events. This is what accounts for so many reactions to adversity.

We used to keep a permanent reminder of this concept around our house. My young son, Paul, was playing with his Big Wheel in the backyard, except that his Big Wheel had just one wheel. The toy had broken at the neck and all that was left was the big front wheel attached to the handle bars. It looked like a unicycle with handlebars. I felt bad for him and asked if he wanted to go to the store and buy a new one.

He said, "No Dad. It's okay. I like my One Wheeler."

I said, "One Wheeler?"

Paul responded, "Yeah. I've got a One Wheeler. I can take it anywhere—in the sand box, around the swing set, up and down the hill—and besides, Dad, I'm the only one in the neighborhood who has a One Wheeler."

I stood there agape. I saw a broken toy; my son saw a unique toy. The One Wheeler hung in the garage for years, as a visual reminder to me that there is more than one way to process life. I drew from his optimism.

Is a downturn in business a tragedy, or is it an opportunity for you and your company to demonstrate your persistence, creativity, and "grace under pressure"? Could it be an opportunity for you to prove to your customers that you are committed to their business, especially in tough times? When the customer challenges your price, is it an objection, or a request for information on why your package is worth your price?

9. Do things that bring you joy

Give yourself a mental break and enjoy the trip. I was playing in a golf tournament recently and saw one of my customers on the golf course. His company is an industrial distributor in a market that is going through some tough times right now. He joked matter-of-factly, "Might as well play golf. We can't sell anything." Then he laughed and hit a pretty good shot. This is not permission to skip work and go out and play golf, but it does illustrate my point. In tough times, it is important to do things that still bring you joy. You need the break.

During the year I spent in combat, the U.S. Army offered troops an R&R (rest and recuperation) to get away from the fighting. We could go to Thailand, Australia, or even Hawaii for a few days. Some of us chose to take an in-country R&R for a rest. This was a well-deserved respite for us. Everyone needs to break loose and relax.

Stress management experts emphasize the importance of exercising during tough times to experience the endorphin release—nature's remedy for a trip down in the dumps. Endorphins make you feel better.

> ➢ Any time you do something positive for yourself, you begin to feel better.

If reading at the library gives you joy, go to the library. If riding your bike five miles makes you feel better, start peddling. If playing golf is your hobby, hack away. Regenerating your body and mind will prepare you for the heavy lifting in your job. It also adds a dimension of normalcy to tough times.

10. Celebrate success

Feel good about your accomplishments. Celebrate them. It's good for the soul and great for your mind. Every success carries with it an educational and motivational benefit. Success inspires as it educates.

Ted Williams appeared on television, and the interviewer asked him what it felt like the year he hit 400-plus. He said, "What I remember most from that year is how I would lie awake in bed at night and think about my hitting streak. The baseball looked as big as a basketball coming over home plate; I couldn't miss it. My logic was simple. If I didn't know what I was doing right when I was doing it right, how would I know what to do right when I was doing it wrong?" He learned from his success. That's the educational benefit of success.

Emotionally, it's good to reflect on your successes. You feel bad when you fail, don't you? Why not enjoy your successes? You deserve the credit. Use this positive energy as fuel to get up tomorrow morning and give it another run. Leverage one success into another. How many times have you heard, "The best time to make a sale is right after you make a sale"? The reason is that the principles of success that work uniquely for you are in place, mentally and emotionally. You are enjoying the thrill of success.

As a professional speaker, there are some days that are more fun than fun. On those days particularly, I will sit back and ask myself why the day's activities were so effortless. In fact, I have so much fun on these days that I find it remarkable that I get paid for it. I want to reflect on the day, bask in the good feelings, and understand that little bit of magic that made the day special. Then, I can sprinkle some of that magic in my next presentation.

If I were your personal sales coach, I would invest time helping you to understand and enjoy your successes. Within you is a great success story waiting to be written on the streets with your performance. Start writing.

11. Leave a bigger woodpile than the one you found when you came into this world

A friend of mine, Denis Waitley, is fond of saying, "Plant a shade tree under which you will never sit." The premise of this concept is to get the focus off you and on to what you can do for others. It's difficult to wallow in self-pity when you're focused on giving back in some fashion. This shift in your mindset directs your energy outward.

Viktor Frankl, whom I quoted earlier, wrote *Man's Search for Meaning* about his experiences in Nazi concentration camps. He discovered that those who survived in these camps had a higher calling to do something or give something back when set free. Prior to their release, they felt the need to contribute. It's one of the things that helped them sustain themselves in the most abysmal conditions any of us can imagine.

Therapists use the term autovectoral to describe the phenomenon when you are primarily focused on yourself—all vectors are directed towards you. Allovectoral means that you are primarily focused on the other person—all vectors lead to them.

> ➤ When you leave a bigger woodpile than the
>   one you found, you're in the giver mode,
>   not the taker mode—you're focused on others
>   versus yourself.

You're attempting to make a difference, which means you're action oriented—one of the prerequisites of lifting yourself out of tough times. You will find it difficult to preoccupy yourself with worry and stress as you plant these shade trees and build bigger woodpiles. You're in a positive mode, which brings positive outcomes.

12. Play to win

Are you playing to win, or are you playing just hard enough not to lose? Never is this difference so obvious as in tough times. Tough timers play to win all the time. They waste little time looking over their shoulders.

> ➤ Those who play not to lose focus on basic
> survival; those who play to win focus their
> energy and time on thriving.

Two of my clients, each faced with similar market conditions, approach their adversity as differently as two people can. I talked to one company's CEO, and he sounded as if the wake for his company were tomorrow. His mood was gloomy, and his view of the economy was gloomier. He saw little hope for the future. His conversation was a morose display of poor leadership. Two weeks before this conversation, I talked to another company's leader whose business was off 50% for the year; he was investing in technology, training his salespeople, and retooling for the future. He was optimistic about the future and viewed this slowdown as an opportunity to get better. He was playing to win; the other CEO was playing not to lose.

Tiger Woods epitomizes the tough timer. In 2000, he won a major golf tournament at Pebble Beach by fifteen strokes! He needed one stroke to win, but decided he would play to his potential, not just against the rest of the field. In 2001, he won the Master's tournament similarly. On the 18th hole, he had a one-stroke lead and was staring at a ten-foot putt. Since he was in the last group to come in, all he had to do was sink the putt in two stokes, and he could win the tournament. Not Tiger. He sank the putt and finished two strokes ahead of the pack. He played to win, not just not to lose. Are you playing hard enough to win or just hard enough not to lose?

Mind food

I've included some thoughts here that I draw strength from, and hope you find strength and optimism in these words also. Knowing that you're not the first salesperson to confront tough times helps, but you need not reinvent the wheel. Each offers hope so that you may find the strength to get up in the morning, lick your wounds, and fight another day.

Tough times never last; tough people do.

Robert Schuller

Any fact facing us is not as important as our attitude toward it, for that determines our success or failure.

Norman Vincent Peale

Experience is not what happens to a man; it is what a man does with what happens to him.

Aldous Huxley

What we do not see, what most of us never suspect of existing, is the silent but irresistible power which comes to the rescue of those who fight on in the face of discouragement.

Napoleon Hill

All things are difficult before they are easy.

Thomas Fuller

If you can force your heart and nerve and sinew to serve your turn long after they are gone, and hold on when there is nothing in you except the Will which says to them: "Hold on!"

Rudyard Kipling

They can . . . because they think they can.

Virgil

Everything is possible for him who believes.

Mark 9:23

The pressure of adversity does not affect the mind of the brave man . . . it is more powerful than external circumstances.

Seneca

Your ability will stretch to your capacity for believing.

Tom Reilly

Summary

We move in the direction of our thoughts, and attitude drives behavior. We behave as we believe. This section was about how you fight the battle in your mind during tough times. Positive mental programming is how you talk to yourself to set yourself up for success. Those who prevail in tough times demonstrate courage, understand the limited scope of the problem, feel they can control their destiny, feel they can make a difference, rely on their creativity for possibilities, and persevere until they win.

3
Selling in Tough Times

Success is to be measured not so much by the position
that one has reached in life as by the obstacles
which he has overcome while trying to succeed.
Booker T. Washington

You're fighting the battle in your head and winning. Now it's time to fight the battle on the streets. This chapter gives you practical and street-smart ideas for behind-the-scenes and front-line selling activities.

Behind-the-scenes strategies for tough times

1. Get the pressure off yourself

As a salesperson, you face pressure on three fronts: your company, your customers, and your personal life. Get the pressure off yourself personally, and free up that energy to use positively to fight your battle on the streets. Tough times selling requires all the positive energy you can muster. Reduce spending for the niceties, not the necessities. Get rid of bills. Hold off spending more than you need to spend. Can you modify vacation plans? How about dinner at a sports bar versus a five-star restaurant? Can you play with your old golf clubs another season?

I know a salesperson who recently lost his job but plunged ahead, spending as if he had just gotten a promotion. He had a small severance package and spent $15,000 of it remodeling his kitchen. A few months passed before he got a job. He discovered this expenditure had the opposite effect he had hoped for. It added to his stress versus his enjoying a modern kitchen.

Getting the pressure off yourself is common sense advice, but most people need to be reminded of this from time to time.

> ➢ Spend prudently and invest in those areas that
>   you can leverage into a greater opportunity.

To paraphrase an old saying, when you have more time than money, leverage your time. When you have more money than time, invest your money to gain more time. In tough times, you may have more time than money to invest. Invest both prudently.

2. Prepare-prepare-prepare

In tough times, there is a narrow margin for mistakes. More people are competing for the limited amount of business. You cannot afford to shoot yourself in the foot with sloppiness. Your attention to detail is paramount to success. Review quotes and proposals. Make sure everything is correct. Rehearse your presentations. Plan your sales calls, realizing that price may be an issue. Prepare your list of questions and benefits that will shift the focus off price and onto cost-saving benefits.

In tough times, you can link your attitude to good planning for success. Hope for the best, and plan for the worst. Be prepared. Set reasonable and challenging goals. Goals excite. You may need to revamp your goals for tough times, but you still need a target to shoot for. Far-reaching goals that are unreasonable frustrate and discourage you. Inspire yourself with realistic goals that encourage you to stretch. Fewer than one in four salespeople have a detailed plan of attack for their number one account. This is an opportunity area for you. If your competition does not plan and you do, it gives you an advantage over them.

> ➤ Planning and preparation result
> in twice the performance.

Have a list of rebuttals prepared for price objections. Know what you will say when the buyer says, "Your price is too high." Know what you will say if the buyer says, "We just can't do anything now." If you've done your homework and prepared for the sales call, you might respond with something like, "Do you know what will happen if you choose to do nothing to get the jump on this problem? Nothing."

3. Practice good time management

You may find that you have more of this valuable resource available in tough times. It's important to treat time with the same respect as you do in good times. Invest your time prudently in areas that will give you the return you seek. You may work longer hours in tough times. Consider the alternative. Would you rather work longer hours or no hours in tough times? You must work smarter in tough times. Invest your time where you get the greatest return. Understand priorities and set them by payoff, not urgency. Work on your effectiveness. Effectiveness is doing the right things. Efficiency is doing things the right way.

> ➤ There is nothing so useless as doing things efficiently that shouldn't be done at all.
>
> Peter Drucker

Tough times present you with gifts of time. Gifts of time are those unexpected moments during the day when you did not anticipate extra time. For example, a gift of time is the extra twenty minutes a customer keeps you waiting. What do you do with that time? Some salespeople use it to thumb through magazines. Others use it to review their notes for their presentations.

Like most major corporations recently, Corning has been experiencing tough times, especially in their high-tech markets. Their CEO, John Looses, who has weathered many of these storms in the past, said that it was a good time to go back and examine their manufacturing processes. "I've been here for thirty-seven years and on the senior management team for fourteen years. We've been through this before. If you panic, the organization will panic and lose effectiveness . . . However, you have to be realistic and prepare for the worst case. We have contingency plans assuming (the economy) will not come out of this until well into 2002. We're not saying that in six months we'll be right back at it. You want to keep top people and continue to invest in technology. But this way, you get fixed costs under control." With this strong leadership, is there any question that they will emerge from tough times victorious?

You may even find that tough times brings extra time for you to meet with customers. If a customer doesn't have much going on, he may have more time available to meet with you and discuss what will happen in the future. Tough times give you an opportunity to work on relationship building.

On a personal level, tough times offer you the opportunity to work on personal development. Read. Study. Listen to tapes. When things are rolling, companies may not feel the need to upgrade their employee's performance. Good times hide mediocre performance. Tough times spotlight it.

Face-to-face selling strategies

1. Be a positive information source

Your customer is inundated with bad news. They are surrounded by the bad news bears. You may be the only sunshine they see today. I met a salesperson who was long in the tooth, and he said to me, "If the sun is not shining, I better be." This was his way of saying that he needed to bring sunshine to the customer. If every salesperson who calls on the buyer is negative and you're positive, whom do you think the customer will want to see?

> ➤ You must be a hope merchant.
> Spread your message of hope far and wide.
> Customers are eager to buy it.

Inform the customer about your company's plans for growth in the future—your investments in technology that will have a positive impact on their business. Share your knowledge of the future of the industry in a positive way. Tell the customer how other companies are using slow times to lay the ground work for expansion, once tough times are over. Offer cost containment and profit enhancement ideas. Profit enhancement is a different mindset than cost cutting. Cost cutting means doing less of something; profit enhancement could imply doing more of something that will boost the bottom line. Sell your customer on the concept of profit enhancement, especially if they must invest money in your product to achieve their profit goals.

Keep your tone positive and your message optimistic. The customer may depend on you for a desperately needed shot in the arm. If you pack some hope in your briefcase and share it freely with others, you may discover the buyer wants you to come around more often in tough times.

2. Sell value, not price

The temptation to cut your price in tough times is great. If you cut your price, how will you get your prices up when the tough times are over? Stay on message. Stay the course. You have been successful with your value added all along. Now is not the time to change your message. Your value doesn't diminish in tough times. Why should your price go down? Your value added may be more important to the customer in tough times because they need maximum value for their money.

If you need a shot in the arm, go back and review your list of value added to remind yourself of why your company is strong. Talk to existing customers who appreciate everything you do. It's great spiritual fuel. They may offer a hint why other companies should focus on your value, not the price.

3. Promise a lot and deliver more

Focus on delivering more than you promise. This is essential for customer satisfaction. In tough times, you cannot afford dissatisfied customers. You can't afford dissatisfied customers in good times, for that matter. By focusing on delivering more than you promise, you are putting the customer first. It reinforces their decision to buy. They feel better about the money they spend with you. Reassure buyers in tough times. Rely on your guarantees of complete satisfaction. You are guaranteeing their money's worth. Buyers want to feel that they make good decisions. Delivering more than you promise reinforces this buying decision. Exceeding their expectations builds customer satisfaction.

4. Lose no business

Similarly, nail shut your back door. On average, it costs ten times more to get a new customer than to keep an existing customer happy. The cost skyrockets in tough times because fewer people are buying. Competitors will aggressively pursue your installed base of business in tough times. They will try to steal, by any means, what you have in place. Make a pledge to yourself that you will lose no business. Begin your defensive selling campaign to shore up your existing business.

> ➤ Treat your customers as if they were
> prospects—they are, for the competition.

In quality control training, they teach about zero defects. This means error-free performance. Defensive selling means zero defections. It's working as hard to keep the business as you did to get the business. Defensive selling is the sale-after-the-sale. Document your value added, brag positively about the value you deliver, and conduct customer satisfaction sales calls. Your goal is to be so good and deliver so much value that the customer cannot afford *not* to do business with you.

5. Make more calls

Earlier in this book, I discussed the three biggest mistakes that salespeople make in tough times. One of them was that they reduce face-to-face calling by 38% in tough times. Increasing your face-time with customers by 25% enables you to effectively double your coverage. In tough times, you must work harder. There is no way to sugarcoat it. The forty-hour work week is not sacrosanct.

When I fought in a war, we flew seven days a week. Weekends were something we left behind with our civilian clothes. Under normal conditions, I'm a huge believer in off-time. As the saying goes, desperate times require desperate actions. If you're in a battle for survival, you may need to put in more hours than you normally work. And that's okay for a limited time. I don't advocate workaholism. This is also why it's important to balance your life. Do things that bring you joy, and make time for regeneration. If you're working harder, you will need to get away and erase the blackboard.

I have used a rule of thumb for years. I make it a habit to talk to three people every non-speaking day about a new piece of business. Maintaining this activity level produces for me a steady flow of business. In tough times, I may bump this number to five people per day—a 67% increase in my calling efforts. It's important to stay ahead of the curve. Increase your calling efforts and fill your pipeline before it becomes a crisis.

> ➤ Fewer people buy in tough times; those who do buy move slower. It requires more effort to fill the pipeline.

Making more calls means you may have to arrive at the office earlier to handle paperwork that you would normally handle during prime calling hours. It could mean that you meet a customer for breakfast or dinner. You may decide to stay late and design your proposals in the late afternoon hours when there are fewer distractions around the office. As your competition looks for ways to avoid the inevitable rejection that accompanies tough times, you're out there filling their time slots. You're doubling your coverage. Few things will slip through the cracks. The orders may be smaller, but they will be your smaller orders.

6. Don't let the customer see you sweat

Customers always speak on the record. Customers will use anything you say in their negotiation. If customers know your business is faltering, they will use this information to gain negotiating momentum. When the customer asks how your business is doing, there is only one word for you to respond with, "Incredible," because it covers all contingencies. Few words allow you to say so much and so little at the same time. You really haven't said anything, but you have answered the customer's question.

Some salespeople feel the need to share all of their problems with customers. This is a bad negotiating strategy. Do you feel the need to tell the customer when you have an ingrown toenail? If you're constipated, would you share that with customers? Why do you feel the need to tell the customer if your sales are off? They are listening for that information. You don't have to lie to customers, but you can understate the impact on your company. "We're watching our expenses like everyone else; that's just good economic policy. We do that in good times, too. But we're moving forward with our investments in technology and R&D. We want to be ready to help you move forward when the economy turns."

Some argue that it's important for customers to know if you're struggling. Others argue further that your struggles demonstrate empathy for the customer. And still others point out that if the customer believes your business is too good, they may ask for special help because you're doing fine. In the words of one of my customer's when I sold commodity chemicals, "When the rat race starts, all the rats start scrambling." In other words, if they smell blood, they will move in for the negotiating kill. It is naive for you to believe that if your customer knows you're desperate to sell, they will not use that information in their purchasing. Besides, who really wants to do business with someone who is desperate?

There is no strategic advantage for you to have your customers believe you're hurting. This may cause them to direct business to a competitor who they feel is not hurting; the customer may not want the vulnerability of directing too much of their business to a company that is struggling. Beyond that, they may tell the competition why they are shifting business to them, and you know what the competition will do with that information.

7. Empathize, don't sympathize

This is more than a game of semantics; it's a difference in your attitude. Empathy is the intellectual understanding of someone's pain. Sympathy is when you sit down and cry with the customer. There must be no false sense of duty on your part to bleed when someone else is cut. You can understand their pain without cutting yourself. Maintain your objectivity and professional distance. They are your customers, and you do have strong obligations to them. But you also have strong obligations to your company.

If you cross the empathy/sympathy line, you may relent on your pricing and cave in to their price objections.

Understand their pain, but hold the line. You are not responsible for their tough times. You can help the customer in many ways, but hold the line on profitability. If your company were experiencing tough times, would the customer tell you it's okay to raise your prices beyond normal price increases because you're struggling and need help? Not in this lifetime!

8. *Leverage every opportunity*

In good times and tough times, successful people leverage every opportunity. Leveraging is achieving a high ratio of outcome to input. Expand your penetration vertically and horizontally. Sell deep and wide into your accounts. Are you getting full account penetration? Are there other things this customer should be buying from you? Do they have other locations that you could sell to? Does this buyer know other people outside of their organization you can talk to? What are the evolutionary spin-offs to your products? Leave no stone unturned in your search for business.

Selling to existing customers is more cost-effective and quicker than selling to prospects. When customers buy more products from you, it saves them money to cut fewer purchase orders. It costs your company less to process several items for one customer versus one item for several customers. It takes seven calls to close a new customer on a new idea and three calls to close an existing customer on the same new idea.

9. Influence and lead

There are leaders and there are followers; someone must lead and someone must follow. Which will you be? You don't have to be a manager to be a leader. Most sales forces have salespeople who possess great leadership traits and inspire others around them with their optimism and hope. Enthusiasm plays a major role in your persuasiveness. How can you expect customers to get excited about what you sell if you're not excited about it?

> ➢ Customers want to deal with leaders,
> not followers.

Be an opinion leader. Spread hope and optimism. One of the best examples of this is Winston Churchill when he spoke to a gathering of young men during World War II. He inspired the audience with his leadership in just seven words: "Never, never, never, never, never, never quit."

Be a thought leader for your customers. Take them new ideas and new solutions to old problems. Help them see the rainbow. What people want more than anything else is hope. People want to believe that tough times will pass. Customers will follow you if you bring them hope and lead with your example.

You may find it necessary to share this optimism with your peers and internal customers. Optimists are not depleted of their hope as they share it with others. In fact, the opposite is true. Hope is one of those things that the more you share, the more you get in return. It's the boomerang effect in life—you get back that which you throw out. Thackeray said, "Life is like a mirror. You get back what you put in." As you share hope, you receive hope.

10. Get your manager in the field more

A good management strategy is to visit customers often. In tough times, it's imperative. Your manager can be a source of strength for the marketplace, if he or she brings hope and reassurance. It's also important for your manager to see first-hand what you're experiencing. This may help you with your internal battles to get things done. The empathy your boss gains is good for you also.

Be clear before you make the call what you want your manager to say on the sales call. Coordinate your messages. You want to reassure the customer about your commitments to the industry, the quality of your product, and their satisfaction. You want your manager to identify areas where he or she can be of unique service to the customer.

11. Probe for pain and hope

Specifically, probe for root-canal pain. Seek those areas that hurt the buyer more than paying too much for something. Identify buyer pressure points. A pressure point is any condition that mitigates the importance of acquisition price. Make a list of questions that will take the focus off their misery and redirect it to the future.

> ➢ **Everyone hates something
> more than spending money.**

In tough times, buyers find it difficult to focus, as they have many distractions competing for their attention. Narrow the buyer's focus with your questions to target specific areas where they may be able to do something positive. Focused and specific changes are realistic in tough times. Across-the-board changes and enhancements are unrealistic in tough times. Ask about future projects and what their plans are for down the road:

- How do you see things changing as the pace picks up?
- What will be your first priority to work on?
- Where will your first upgrade or investment be when things make a turn?
- Is there one thing right now you would like to improve to make your life easier?
- What are you working on today for tomorrow?
- What do you see being critical for you when your business picks up?

You want the buyer focusing on these issues. If you can get the buyer thinking about the future, you can begin to lay the groundwork for further sales. You want your solution to be in-place when the spigot opens. You also want to help your company forecast customers' needs. Your internal staff can begin their preparations, depending on your ability to get these forecasts.

12. Probe for discretionary dollars

There is always money. It just shifts from account to account, depending on the most pressing needs at the moment. I work with a manufacturer that has experienced a "depression" in their industry. Their business fell off 50% in one year. They have laid off half their work force and slashed budgets radically across the board. At the same time, they hosted a costly dealer meeting in Las Vegas.

I recently talked to a business owner about a training assignment, and he told me how tough things had become in his industry: layoffs, production cuts, across-the-board cost reductions, and scrapped projects. He was singing the blues about his business. In his next breath, he told me about a ten-day Caribbean vacation he was taking the next month. Business couldn't have been too bad.

> ➤ There is always money. It just moves from one account to another, depending on the buyer's shifting priorities.

Buying and selling is all about priorities. But you must penetrate the account at the highest possible level to find the money. Never take "No" from someone who cannot say, "Yes." High-level decision makers have the authority to approve funding for an idea they like; in tough times, they like ideas that help swell their bottom lines. Most groups that I work with do not have enough "zeroes" in their prices to frighten high-level decision makers.

One question I've found useful to ask is, "It's been my experience that there are generally discretionary dollars available to move from one account to another, depending on the most pressing need. Is that the case here?" After you ask this question, pause and let your buyer respond. That becomes your target area for funding.

13. Focus long term

Always view success in the long term and failure in the short term. You are on the road to success. You are doing all of those things that successful people do. You may encounter bumps along the way—I would be surprised if you didn't. Your failures are short term; your successes are spread over the long term. This focus helps you maintain your positive mental attitude when things get tough, and it gives you a useful backdrop to work with customers.

Continue to focus on long-range issues with customers. Their short-term pain will end as soon as the spigot opens and they can begin the projects that are currently on hold. This long-range focus also enables you to discuss the long-term relationship that you have established with the customer and how that will continue in the future.

14. *Keep your emotions under control*

It's impossible to deal with other people's emotions unless your emotions are under control. In tough times, everyone is stressed. You have the normal stress of day-to-day living compounded by a weak economy or some other adversity. Tempers run short and emotions run high. Whoever handles stress more effectively emerges victorious from tough times.

In tough times, you may need to demonstrate a greater tolerance for others' emotions. When someone is rattled and the person they interact with maintains his or her composure, the anxious person draws strength and tranquility from the calm person. You may represent the only stability in the buyer's world. Share your emotional control with the buyer. Lead with your courage—your "grace under pressure"—and listen with your heart.

15. *Continue with your proactive message*

Talk about the investments that your company is making in R&D, the quality initiatives, and financial stability of your company. One company I worked with continued to reinvest in R&D, even in the darkest hours of their industry's downturn. Everyone in the industry knew this. Everyone respected this company for their commitment to excellence and leadership in the market. When the economy improved for their industry, this company was perched for growth. They had a one-year marketing window to capture the early, profitable business opportunities because everyone wanted to take advantage of their innovations. It took the competition that long to catch up. By then, this company launched its next level of innovations, which expanded their competitive gap.

16. Be flexible

You may discover that in tough times your flexibility, adaptability, and creativity are your greatest allies. Because customers are seeking ways to operate more efficiently to enhance their profits, they may be more open to your innovative ideas. You may find more people willing to visit with you if you're selling creativity and flexibility. A friend of mine sells material handling devices. In good times, his customers expand horizontally by building new facilities. In tough times, they expand vertically by using overhead space. They grow in good times and become more efficient in tough times.

> ➢ Tap into your company's versatility in meeting customer demands for growth and efficiency.

People may decide to keep equipment longer and survive by repairing the old equipment. Focus on repair. In the early 1990's, the construction industry suffered a downturn, and a lot of equipment sat idle on dealers' lots. Some dealers started a daily rental program to stimulate cash flow and created a whole new market in the construction equipment industry that is thriving today—daily rental and leasing. In tough times, some of my clients prefer to hear this message of hope, *How to Sell and Manage in Tough Times and Tough Markets*, versus some of the other programs we offer. We adapt to their needs. These are all examples of the evolutionary spin-off opportunities that I discussed earlier in leveraging. In tough times, customers have a short-term time horizon, and they want some immediate relief to make the pain go away. You may have to adapt your solution to this.

17. Create buying opportunities

One of my clients evaluated their inventories and sought ways to free up cash flow. They positioned the campaign as "buying opportunities" for customers. Because they positioned it as a buying opportunity for customers, the customers did not perceive this as an across-the-board discount or a policy change in the seller's pricing or way of doing business. This one-time offer gave customers a chance to stock up and the supplier a way to trim unnecessary inventory while improving their cash position. Once they trimmed the unnecessary inventory, they replaced it sparingly.

Summary

Half the battle is in your head, and the other half is on the streets. This section was about your battle on the streets—selling skills. I offered behind-the-scenes tips to prepare you for your calls. I also offered some ideas for what you can do on the sales call. In tough times, you must work harder and smarter. You must increase your face-time with customers, and be prepared for the inevitable price objections you will hear. Buyers will try to use bad economic news to their negotiating advantage. Be prepared for this.

4

Managing in Tough Times

*Leadership is the art of accomplishing
what the science of management says is possible.*
General Colin Powell
Chairman, Joint Chiefs of Staff

This section is for managers or anyone who wants to think and act like a manager. An important part of management—whether it's territory management or the management of a sales force—is your leadership ability. Are you a good leader? In tough times, we need *great* leaders. A rule of thumb for managers is: *Manage the process and lead your people.* Managers focus on process, and leaders focus on people. This chapter is about leadership under fire. We examine the four biggest mistakes that managers make in tough times, and the seventeen things managers must do in tough times. If you are to lead your organization in and out of tough times, you must become a strong, positive leader.

Leadership in tough times

As we begin this chapter on management and leadership in tough times, I'm struck by the amazing similarities of running a business in tough times and going through a business start-up. Having experienced several of both, I've seen first-hand the impact of effective management and strong leadership. Tough times, as well as start-ups, require vision, passion, courage, economy, discipline, and commitment. As a manager, you focus on the efficiency of your systems and processes. As a leader you focus on people. You inspire them with your vision, infuse them with your passion, impress them with your courage, and ask for their commitment to a disciplined approach to growth and economy. During tough times, you need both dynamics— economy and growth—working for you. Manage the process, but lead your people.

In tough times, your employees and customers look to you for stability and hope. They will take their lead from you. If you panic, they panic. If you demonstrate "grace under pressure," they will draw security from your wellspring of strength. Your performance under fire will determine the future of your organization.

> ➤ Leaders inspire others to act. They make other people believe that the impossible is possible. They set the tone for others to follow.

As a strong leader under fire, you must communicate your vision for the future. People want to feel optimistic that "this, too, shall pass." They want you to share your vision of the future—where the problems they currently face are solved. They want to draw from your confidence in your ability to turn this thing around and prevail. As a leader, you don't have the luxury of wilting under fire. You have to be stronger than everyone else so they can tap into your strength. If you doubt the importance of this dynamic, talk to those who have led people out of tough times. They will tell you that, as a leader, you set the tone for thriving that everyone else follows.

Employees and customers expect you to be empathic to their concerns but not incapacitated by them. Empathy helps you feel what they're going through, and this insight provides a moral compass for the direction your decisions take. Trust plays a major role in leading your people in tough times. They must feel your motives are noble. If they trust you, they will implement your policies and procedures without hesitation. They know in their hearts you're acting out of a genuine concern for the organization and its future, which is also their future. Empathy also means you share the pain.

> ➢ Pain must start at the top. If you're not feeling the same pain your employees feel, it's one-sided pain.

Trust, integrity, confidence in your competence, strength under pressure, and empathy for those whom you lead. Employees and customers want to see these attributes in their leaders. Share your dreams. Share your confidence. Share their burdens. Inspire them with your leadership.

Four biggest mistakes managers make in tough times

Like salespeople, managers make mistakes in tough times. From our research, we've identified the four biggest mistakes managers make in tough times. Recognizing and understanding these mistakes can help you avoid some of the pitfalls many managers face.

1. Managers believe everything salespeople say

This is similar to the same mistake salespeople make with customers. When managers believe everything salespeople tell them, it biases their decisions. As a leader, you must listen to your troops—employees and customers. Hear them and use this as part of your intelligence operation for making decisions. One-dimensional decisions are short-sighted. This is one reason to spend more time in the field—to hear what your customers are saying about their needs, the marketplace, the competition, and their customers. Base forecasts on solid market information, not just sales force input. Their input is important but not absolute. It will always contain a sales bias. Balance this with other department's feedback. Meeting with other departments and a cross section of customers broadens your information base and gives you the opportunity to share a different point of view with your salespeople.

2. Radical cost slashing

When cutting costs, prudently prune expenses instead of using across-the-board slashing. When you cut costs across the board, you slash funding in areas that are vital to your success. For example, do you really want to slash marketing budgets when you need more business? Do you want to lose top employees because your slashing may deplete their department of the valuable resources they need to perform their jobs successfully? Surgical strikes are more efficient and targeted. They achieve greater success because of your concentrated effort on hot spots, and they achieve objectives with minimal casualties.

> ➤ Across-the-board budget cuts are like blanket bombing; you get the job done but leave too much collateral damage in your wake.

Ask employees where they perceive waste. They are closer to the action and can identify waste quickly. Asking them for their input also involves them in the process so that they are committed to your efforts. They develop an understanding of where and how you're attempting to tighten your belts strategically. Using their input removes some of their legitimate fears about losing their jobs.

3. Reduced promotional efforts

It's common business practice that the advertising budget is the first budget to go in tough times. Why? If your advertising results are questionable, you should cut the campaign before tough times just out of good business policy. Cutting effective campaigns during tough times is shooting yourself in the foot. You're canceling your method for attracting new customers. It's like a thirsty man deciding that he will reduce his need for water by reducing his overall activity level, even when one of his key activities is walking to the well to draw water.

In tough times, the noise level for advertising goes down significantly. A Cahners Publishing Company study estimates that those who increase their marketing activity in tough times outperform the industry average for market share gain by 2½ times the rate other companies grow. And they get a rebound effect for two years after the tough times. When everyone else cuts back and you maintain your investments in advertising and promotion, you may effectively double your exposure for the same amount of money. Increasing investments in this area gives your company even greater exposure. You gain share and reinforce a positive image in the customers' minds.

4. No tough times plan

This is like driving by looking in the rear view mirror. Some are unprepared for tough times, and they scramble to adjust course. Telling you about this when you're in tough times is like telling you that you just missed your turn off the highway. Most companies have a disaster plan for emergencies, but few have a plan to thwart tough times. Smart leaders prepare for the worst, hope for better, and focus their companies on what they do best. Their plan is their bridge between dreams and reality—the difference between pain and gain.

Sixteen things you can do in tough times

As a manager, there are things you can do in the midst of tough times to lift your organization to the next level. In tough times, you must get back to the basics of your business—all of those things that got you to where you are today—focusing resources on your core competencies. This list of ideas will help. Read with an open mind.

1. Selective input

Just as salespeople selectively input what they hear from customers, the same advice applies to managers.

> ➤ As a manager, you must listen to your employees; what they perceive as reality is reality for them.

You're dealing with their perceptions of the situation. But their perception is not the full story. You must expand your intelligence network to include customers, other managers, different regions, other departments, and on a broader scale, industry and non-industry sources. Your department or region may be waging a war that is different than a department in another part of the country. It's useful to get another manager's input to check your assumptions. Avoid one dimensional decisions.

2. Make prudent cost-containment decisions

As I mentioned earlier in this section, managers err when they slash costs in a blanket sweep to reduce expenditures. Targeted cuts in nonessential areas ideally cut fat. If you must cut costs, ask your folks where they think you should cut costs. They are closer to the action and will give you good feedback. I've heard some creative ways lately for how companies are cutting costs. Xerox found that if employees at one of their offices paid 25¢ for each cup of coffee, it would save one employee's job. Employees are willing to water plants at Xerox—to the annual savings of $200,000—instead of having a plant watering service take care of it. American Standard found that employees were willing to vacuum their entrance mats—versus sending them out for cleaning—when they discovered it saved the company $70,000 annually. There's the legendary $100,000 olive at American Airlines. During the 1980's, American Airlines found that if they reduced the total number of olives by just one olive per salad, they would save $100,000 per year; no customers noticed the missing olive. Another company decided that if everyone would take a 5% salary reduction, it could save 5% of the jobs. The advantage of this method is that everyone shares in the pain. You may even shorten the work week to thirty-five hours, which reduces salaries across-the-board.

3. Visit customers

As a leader, your job is to reassure others that everything will be okay. Customers will want to know that your business is moving in the right direction. In good times, two-thirds of high-level decision makers report that they want to meet with their high-level counterparts; in tough times, that number increases. Reassure your staff and customers that you have strategic plans in place to deal with the current downturn. You must demonstrate the "this, too, will pass" attitude, and share it with everyone inside and outside your organization.

4. Don't shoot the messenger

Sophocles said, "Nobody likes the man who brings bad news." Throughout history, kings shot messengers when they didn't like the news the messengers brought. You don't have the luxury of hearing only the news that you want to hear. Your accounting department may have a different outlook than your sales department. Listen to them. Make sure your folks know they can come to you with their concerns and you will give them an audience. Here's a bonus! If they feel they can approach you with their concerns, employees may bring new ideas for old problems.

5. Increase promotions

This may be the hardest advice for you to accept because it involves money leaving your company. Yet, this counter-intuitive strategy pays huge dividends. The noise level is lower in tough times; your exposure is higher.

> ➢ **Three out of four companies reduce marketing expenditures in tough times.**

Increasing promotional efforts includes every way you communicate with customers, not just advertising. Correspondence to customers can be an effective way to communicate. Check media sources for remnant space. This is last-minute space they have available that they want to fill. Increase field sales exposure; tell your salespeople to increase their face-time by 25%. Redeploy other employees into promotional capacities to support your sales efforts.

6. Think like a farmer

In the winter months, farmers work on equipment and other aspects of their business that they typically ignore during planting and harvesting. They assign seasonal priorities. You may find that slow times are ideal for retrofitting your facility, examining your production processes, training your people, and adjusting inventory. You may want new systems in place for when the economy turns and you experience an increase in volume.

Tough times require companies to become more efficient. Some business strategists and economists even argue the tough times are necessary for progress—innovation is at the heart of efficiency. Contractions have a bright side if you view them in this light. We're in a period now that is like the day after eating at a smorgasbord. You are full but know that you will eat again. You may even diet for a few days, but you will eat again. Our economy will expand again—it always does.

7. Focus on teams

Tempers run short in tough times. People are on edge. Part of leadership is maintaining the cohesiveness of your teams. With all of the competition you have on the streets, you don't need competition inside your walls. Team members must support each other, especially in tough times.

Salespeople are easy targets in tough times because they are the revenue streams for most organizations. Other employees may feel that the sales department is not doing its job, which explains why the company is experiencing tough times. As the leader, you must quash that attitude immediately. In tough times, you need all team members supporting each other and directing this synergy at the marketplace. Tough times require tough teams.

> ➢ Team members must build each other up, not break each other down.

8. Eliminate work, not people

The premise behind most reorganizations is that there is fat in the work force. That may be true. But does the fat exist in the form of weak employees or unnecessary jobs? If the problem is weak employees, you don't need tough times to tell you to get rid of them. You should have already done that. Failing to do so is the result of poor management practices. If it's unnecessary work being performed by good employees, redirect them and place these folks in mission-critical positions. Tough times spotlight the "fat," and it becomes more obvious; it was there in good times also.

Customer and employee loyalty are key drivers of a company's profitability. Loyal employees show up for work, work hard, and satisfy customers. Loyal customers return with their friends. Employee loyalty drives costs down. Customer loyalty increases revenue. Combined, they drive profitability.

9. Use non-monetary rewards

Money is only one motivator. It's the easiest reward to administer because it requires little time investment by managers. However, in tough times money may be in short supply. What are some other things you can use to reinforce your workers? Praise, recognition, promotions, job enrichment, appreciation dinners, professional development opportunities, and equipment upgrades (computers and vehicles) represent ways that managers can demonstrate their appreciation for a job well done. Because everyone is motivated by different things, use a variety of these reinforcers.

10. Develop a proactive credit policy

Stay ahead of receivables unless you want to get into the banking business. If your company is in a cash-rich position, you may want to selectively leverage that strategic advantage with customers who need help on terms. Some customers may be willing to do business with you, and even pay a higher price for your goods and services, if you offer them flexibility in this area.

One of my clients in the heavy equipment industry found that they were able to charge more for their construction equipment if they offered creative payment plans for their customers. One of their customers wanted to purchase an expensive piece of equipment but worried that he might have difficulty making the payments during periods of slower cash flow, so the seller devised a payment schedule that paralleled his periods of high cash flow. The customer paid more for the equipment because of this convenience.

11. Empathize with vendors

Your suppliers are feeling the pinch right now, too. That's the domino effect in business; they're in the trenches with you. Take it easy on them. They are your partners, not the enemy. Try not to use tough times as a way to draw that last bit of blood from their veins. Remember, you will need to work with them after tough times pass. They hope you show them the same consideration you want your customers to show you. Do you have resources you can offer suppliers in tough times to spread the cost and share the benefit?

12. Cut from the top first

If you ask your folks to feel the pain, it must start at the top. Top-down cuts inspire trust and respect in employees. This gives you a sense of empathy for their struggles. If they know you are feeling the pain, they will more readily accept your measures. Unless management foregoes its bonuses and executive privileges, it's unreasonable to expect employees to feel the pain. The great generals throughout history starved with their troops, weathered the same storms, and experienced much of what their armies experienced. Robert E. Lee, one of the most respected generals on both sides of the war, avoided the trappings of his position and lived as his troops lived. This was one of the things that built trust among the ranks. When employees see that you're cutting back personally, as they are cutting back, you gain credibility and their respect.

13. Communicate openly with your employees

They need to know realistic assessments of what is going on in the business. At their levels, they sense what's happening. They need to hear it from you personally. Share the bad news and the good news. Enlist their support with your openness. Everyone must be involved in profit enhancement—revenue production and cost containment. Seek their ideas and input. No one has a monopoly on good ideas, and all good ideas do not originate from the top. Let them know your door and your mind are open.

14. Encourage creativity

You may find that creativity is your greatest ally in tough times. As a rookie salesman, I remember that one of our salespeople found a creative use for one of the expensive solvents we sold. It pushed him over the top in sales and gave the rest of us an idea that helped our division reach its aggressive sales goal that year. Encourage creativity among your salespeople. Ask for new product applications of current technology. Look for evolutionary spin-offs of what you presently offer.

A friend of mine who owns a fastener supply company received the exclusive distribution rights for a fastening device—a brand new technology. He confided in me that he would not have considered this natural spin-off product in good times, but in tough times he had the additional incentive to consider new ideas. His sales will increase during tough times with this product line and soar in good times. He seized the opportunity because he was open to creative ways for boosting revenue. The real bonus is that this new technology is an evolutionary spin-off product.

15. Purge the ranks of cynicism

Get rid of negative salespeople ASAP. You have neither the time or the energy to invest in negativity. They will deplete you of the strength you need to move forward. Additionally, they will infect others in the sales force with their cynicism. Negative salespeople sell less than their positive counterparts. The resources you invest in negative people, wages and benefits, can be redirected into those areas that will give you a better return on your investment. You may find a rebound effect from firing negative people. Other employees may appreciate your actions. They don't like the cynics either.

As a speaker, I deal with negative salespeople in seminars. If you could see the faces of the rest of the group as negative audience members spread their cynicism, you would understand the need to purge your ranks. When I deal with them respectfully and assertively, attempting to redirect their negativity, the group breathes a collective sigh of relief, bordering on applause.

If you are dealing with negativity in the sales force, why in the world would you want negativity in your ranks? What message do you think they are spreading to the customers? They may be badmouthing your company in the presence of customers. Is that the message you want others to hear? Once you make the decision to terminate the negative salesperson, act quickly. Any delay allows their negative energy to serve as a resistance force for the rest of the team. If the rest of the sales force is pulling the wagon as hard as they can, get rid of the freeloaders; they add to the burden.

16. Think forward

Tough times will not last forever. What will your company look like when tough times are over? What are you doing today for tomorrow? Be proactive in developing your vision for the future. Fast forward one year and determine what you need in place to capture the opportunities that will exist when tough times are over. It's difficult to make forward progress when you spend too much time looking over your shoulder.

The Wall Street Journal recently reported that Whirlpool and Intel were both investing huge amounts of money into research and development to help them plot their courses for future business. These two companies happen to be experiencing tough times in their markets, but their leadership is committed to positioning their companies for long-term success as the economy improves. This sounds a lot like Schlumberger, which has an incredible reputation in the oil field service industry for innovative solutions. In the depths of the last oil crunch, their management team pressed forward with their custom of investing 3% of revenue in research and engineering. Is it any wonder they lead the oil field service industry? Their leadership recognized the value of investing in the future, even in tough times.

17. Cash is king

Last but not least. Cash is the lifeblood of organizations. They cannot exist without it. In tough times, it's one of the most precious resources that companies can leverage into competitive gain. Paring surplus inventory, selling obsolete equipment, and pruning expenses are a start. Talk to your banker. Make sure that relationship is sound. You may need their help in tough times to weather the storm or take advantage of a buying opportunity. One high-tech company raised $100 million through an additional stock offering and used that money to finance marketing and product development—moves that will increase their business, regardless of what happens in their high-tech sector.

Coaching in tough times

As a manager, one of the hats you wear is coach. Some people argue that it's the most important hat you wear. In good times, demand is greater than supply and generally masks poor sales performance. Anybody can sell in good times—it's order taking. Tough times spotlight weaknesses in the sales force. Tough times require order making. To lead your organization in and out of tough times, you must spend time with your salespeople.

1. Get out in the field

If you hide in your office, hoping that tough times will go away, tough times will camp on your doorstep until you deal with them. If you sit too long, they will storm into your office. You can't hide from tough times.

> ➢ You can't coach from the locker room.
> You must get in the field with your folks.

How can you give them feedback if all you look at are the numbers? You can fax them a copy of the numbers, if that's the only feedback you're giving. They need qualitative and quantitative feedback. They want to know how they're performing, not just how much they're producing. When you visit them in the field, you can offer behavioral feedback about their performance that may help them achieve their numbers. It gives you something positive to focus on in a sea of negativity. You may find it more motivating in tough times to guide them, not grade them. Build on their strengths, and bring their weaknesses up to an acceptable performance level. You could have good folks performing well, but the numbers don't show it. Do you really want to lose good talent because you only looked at the score card?

Listen to your employees. Salespeople rate "a failure to listen" as their number one complaint about sales managers. The number one reason employees leave their jobs is that they do not like their managers. One study found that 70% of those who left a company rated bad management as their reason for leaving.

2. *Offer reassurance*

People are nervous in tough times. They need reassurance, and they look to their leaders for stability and security. They need to know everything is going to be okay again. Think about flying on a commercial jet. You encounter heavy turbulence—things are bouncing around the cabin. It gets quiet as other passengers consider what's happening. The flight attendants sit down and strap in, and the lady next to you pulls out the rosary. Then, the captain announces over the intercom, "I'm sorry about the bumps, folks. Air traffic control has told us that we will be out of this cell in a couple of minutes, and it should smooth out. Sit back, relax, and enjoy the flight." He says this in a relaxing tone, reassuring as a trusted therapist might reassure a patient. You feel better, don't you? Your employees are the passengers on your corporate jet, and you're the captain. Get on the intercom system, and reassure them that this turbulence will be short lived.

3. *Deal with the fear of failure*

"What if I try and I fail? I don't know if I can take the blow to my self-esteem," the salesman said to me.

I countered, "What if you succeed? How will you know if you never try? Can you really live with that?"

Most people fear failure. Your job is to remind them that failure is a statement about an event, not a judgment about them as a person.

> ➢ Failure is always short term, and success is always long term.

You must coach them that they are responsible for their input, not the outcome of their efforts. Confucius said, "Our greatest glory is not in never failing, but in rising every time we fail." Or as Theodore Roosevelt said, "It is hard to fail, but it is worse never to have tried to succeed."

4. Think motivation

People need a break from tough times. Look for ways to add some fun to their jobs. Add some humor to your staff meetings. Get the edge off of the numbers. I spoke at a meeting where the president of the company introduced me like this: "Ladies and gentlemen, I have good news and bad news. The bad news first. As you know, things are tough in our industry now; we are selling at ninety-seven cents on the dollar. We lose three cents on everything we sell. Now, for the good news. Sales are down this year, so we're not losing as much as we could be losing." He took the edge off a tough situation and made my job easier.

Offer motivational support. Develop themes to stimulate and motivate. Hang motivational posters. Use gifts for creative ideas. Offer "share-in-the-savings" programs for cost-saving ideas. Celebrate successes, no matter how small. Use awards and other recognition programs that let people know you appreciate their efforts.

Adjust sales quotas so that their objectives still motivate your salespeople. Sales targets that are unreasonably high in tough times demotivate. Shift the focus to customer satisfaction and defensive selling objectives which ensure that you will keep the business. Help them see their value to the company. Let them know you appreciate their hard work.

> ➢ As a manager, your job is to make sure the system works. You oversee it. As a leader, you inspire people to want to follow your vision.

You incite them. You make them believe that they can achieve what they may perceive as only possible. As their leader, you may be their beacon in the storm or their navigator for the journey back from the depths of tough times. Are you ready to lead?

Summary

Managers make mistakes in tough times. They believe everything their salespeople tell them, cut costs radically across the board, reduce promotional efforts significantly, and fail to prepare for tough times. Leadership brings companies out of tough times. Leaders demonstrate courage, empathy, and optimism. They give their customers and employees hope for the future. They inspire with their vision. I listed things you can do to lead your company and your employees in and out of tough times.

5

Closing Thoughts

When you get to the end of your rope, tie it in a knot
and hang on with all you've got.
Anonymous

This book has been about personal and professional triumph. We have explored what tough timers do to prevail during adversity. It is a business book that offers ideas that can be generally applied to all areas in our lives.

The human condition is such that we face adversity in all stages of life. No one is immune to tough times in one fashion or another. Trials and tribulations are inescapable for us. Some are great, others pale by comparison. Losing a sale isn't on the same radar screen as losing a loved one; it isn't even close. Losing a sale isn't close to losing one's job. But losing a sale hurts, if you're committed to your career. That tough times are inescapable is one of life's burdens. That we are equipped to confront adversity is one of life's blessings. Humans are hard-wired to detect and react to adversity; it's part of our genetic makeup.

There were several intentionally redundant themes throughout this book. First, you always have a choice for how you perceive life. Perception is the meaning you attach to incoming stimuli. Two people viewing the same life event interpret it differently. One of the great psychological discoveries of our time is that we have the power to change our thinking. Tough timers choose to view adversity as a challenge.

Second, you may not be able to control the outcome of a situation, but you control your input—your thoughts and decisions. Tough timers prevail because they feel responsible for their actions and accountable to themselves. "If it is to be, it's up to me," characterizes their attitude.

Third, your resilience is tied to your creativity and *dream-ability*. You feel more confident as you see endless possibilities for pursuing your goals and confronting your adversity. You are blessed with an imagination and the ability to choose your future. Your ability will expand to your capacity for believing.

Fourth, you are endowed with a strength that enables you to prevail in tough times. It empowers you to hang on, to get up another day, to lick your wounds, and to fight the good fight again and again. It doesn't matter how many times you get knocked down—only that you get up one more time than you are down. As tough times subside, the strength is still there, waiting for you to summon it to come forth and help you prevail in good times.

It is on this last point that I wish to conclude. My purpose in writing this book and sharing these thoughts and experiences with you has been to encourage you to believe that you have within you the power not just to survive, but to thrive in tough times. Beyond tough times and within your reach, using this special power inside you, is your ability to soar above the crowd in good times as well.

It ain't over 'til it's over.

Yogi Berra

About the Author: Tom Reilly

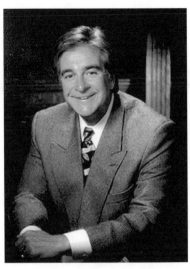

Tom Reilly is president of Tom Reilly Training, a St. Louis based company that specializes in sales and management training.

Tom is uniquely qualified to "lead the way" because of his outstanding sales experience, educational background and success in the training field. He has a Master's Degree in Psychology.

Upon graduating from college, Tom went to work for a Fortune 500 chemical company. In his first year he was their top salesman. He then started his own successful chemical company in Houston, Texas.

In 1981, Tom became a full-time professional speaker and sales trainer. He has trained more than 100,000 salespeople and sales managers in manufacturing, distribution, and the service industries. His client list reads like a "Who's Who" in business.

Tom has authored over forty cassette tapes, a video series, and more than one hundred sales articles. He is also the author of eight hot-selling books: *Value Added Selling, Value Added Sales Management, Value Added Customer Service, Simple Psychology, Crush Price Objections, The Value Added Organization, Selling Smart!,* and *How to Sell and Manage in Tough Times and Tough Markets.*

Books and Tapes by Tom Reilly

Not all readers are leaders, but all leaders must be readers. Harry S Truman

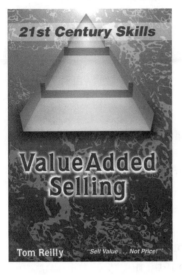

Value Added Selling
The 21st Century Advantage

by Tom Reilly

Value Added Selling is a content-rich message of hope. Whether you are an experienced veteran or a wet-behind-the-ears rookie, you will find this proven customer-oriented sales philosophy a breath of fresh air. It's built on a simple yet profound truth: you can compete successfully and profitably without being the cheapest. **Value Added Selling** teaches you how to sell value, not price. This book launched the value added selling revolution in the 1980s and has been rewritten in 2000 for the twenty-first century. This 26-chapter book offers an in-depth explanation of the value added sales process. It is divided into four sections:

- Section One—Introduction to the value added sales philosophy and what buyers really want from suppliers;
- Section Two—The strategic side of **Value Added Selling**: eleven strategies that value added salespeople use to identify, penetrate, capture, and retain profitable business;
- Section Three—The tactical side of **Value Added Selling**: how to plan and execute the value added sales call;
- Section Four—Bonus section on selling to high-level decision makers, technology, sales letters, and time management.

Book: $24.95   ISBN: 0944448-18-6

Six-audio cassette album: $65.00   ISBN: 0944448-15-1

Contact us: 1-800-727-0026   www.tomreillytraining.com

The Value Added Organization

by Tom Reilly

Organizational excellence is the natural outcome of individual and team excellence. Tom recorded this facilitator-driven, in-house, six-videocassette training series to help organizations introduce their employees to the value added philosophy. The total running time for all six videos is two hours and ten minutes. This translates into nine hours of training and discussion for your employees on how your organization can become a real value added organization. These are some of the important themes covered in this program:

- You and your career: how do you personally add value to your organization's solution?
- You and your peers: how do you add value to your team?
- You and your customers: how do you add value to your relationships with your customers?
- Simply, the way you approach your career, interact with your peers, and interface with your customers determines the level at which your organization competes.

Video series: $600.00 (USD)   ISBN: 0944448-17-8

Book: $10.00   ISBN: 0944448-19-4

Contact us: 1-800-727-0026   www.tomreillytraining.com

Crush Price Objections

Hold the line on prices!

by Tom Reilly

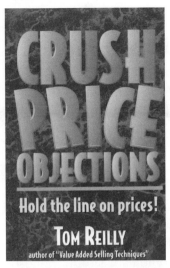

If you're fed up with price resistance, this book is for you. If you want to sell at higher prices, this book is for you. If you want to persist when they resist, this book is for you. This practical street-smart, how-to guide is for anyone that sells in a price-sensitive market. It's divided into three parts:

- Part One—Preparing to sell in a price-sensitive market;
- Part Two—Proactive selling: how to avoid price objections;
- Part Three—How to respond effectively to price objections and negotiate better deals.

Book: $19.95   ISBN: 0-944448-14-3

Two-audio cassette album: $20.00   ISBN: 0944448-16-X

Contact us: 1-800-727-0026   www.tomreillytraining.com

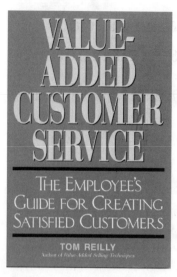

Value Added Customer Service

The Employees Guide
for Creating Satisfied Customers

by Tom Reilly

Customer service is more than a department. It's the attitude that everyone is responsible for customer satisfaction. **Value Added Customer Service** promotes a simple philosophy of exceeding customer expectations and a positive attitude toward serving customers: serving is a privilege, not a pain. In a fiercely competitive world, closing the deal is only part of the solution. Companies that focus on satisfying customers after the sale increase customer loyalty and retention. Those who fail to provide **Value Added Customer Service** scramble to recover the business they lose every year to customer defections. If zero defects is a product quality standard that you aspire to then zero defections must be a customer retention standard that you live by. Here are some of the topics covered in this book:

- Who is responsible for customer satisfaction? Everyone;
- The barriers to effective serving;
- The importance of internal customer service;
- How to deliver **Value Added Customer Service**.

Book: $11.95   ISBN 0-8092-3190-5

Contact us: 1-800-727-0026   www.tomreillytraining.com

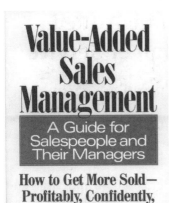

Value-Added Sales Management

A Guide for Salespeople and Their Managers

How to Get More Sold— Profitably, Confidently, and Professionally

TOM REILLY

Value Added Sales Management

Building the Value Added Sales Culture

by Tom Reilly

Sales managers are the change agents for their sales organizations yet most of them are woefully unprepared for the challenge. **Value Added Sales Management** is a comprehensive guide for sales managers—new or experienced. In this book, Tom Reilly shares his insights on having trained more than 100,000 salespeople and their managers. Reilly's motto is simple: "Manage the process and lead your people." He focuses on the critical dynamics of how managers create the value added sales culture and unleash the potential of their sales forces:

- Management and leadership;
- Selection techniques for hiring the best;
- Training and development;
- Establishing sales objectives;
- Coaching for high performance;
- Compensation trends and strategies;
- Motivating plateaued salespeople.

Book: $12.95   ISBN 0-8092-3787-3

Contact us: 1-800-727-0026   www.tomreillytraining.com

Simple Psychology

Simple Living
in a Complex World

by Tom Reilly

Everyone craves simplicity and balance in their complicated lives. **Simple Psychology** is a breath of fresh air in a world crowded with a misery of choices and obligations. It's a return to the values you learned a long time ago and know that ultimately matter. **Simple Psychology** offers spiritual fuel and emotional salve while challenging you to reflect on the choices that you make and how they affect your life and those whom you love. It encourages you to focus on your "being" versus your "having". These are a few of the essays that appear:

- Success is the quality of your journey;
- Can I make a difference?
- Positive mental programming;
- Burdens and blessings;
- Gifts of time.

Book: $19.95   ISBN 0-944448-11-9

Contact us: 1-800-727-0026   www.tomreillytraining.com

Selling Smart

Great Thoughts for Salespeople

by Tom Reilly

Knowledge is power and since 1981 Tom Reilly has been empowering salespeople and their managers with his ideas. Tom has written over one hundred articles for sales, management, and customer service. Tom has selected fifty-nine of his favorites and assembled them in book form. He offers his thoughts in these areas:

- Communications;
- Time management;
- Value Added Selling;
- Attitude;
- Customer service.

Book: $9.95   ISBN 0-944448-09-7

Contact us: 1-800-727-0026   www.tomreillytraining.com